The
Power
of
Colour
to
Heal
the
Environment

Marie
Louise
Lacy

1996

First published in Great Britain in 1996
by Rainbow Bridge Publications
BM Minuet, London WC1N 3XX

ISBN 0-9528700-02
A catalogue record for this book is available from The British Library

Designed by Robin Ollington,
Layout & typography by Frank Lee Associates.

**Cover based on the circle of colour with
the cube representing earth
and the triangle fire, essence
of light within all creation.**

Typeset in 11pt Palatino
with Palatino Bold and Palatino Bold Italic

Printed in Great Britain by
St Edmundsbury Press
Bury St Edmunds
Suffolk IP33 3TU

Dedication

This book is dedicated to all of you who work
with Light and Colour.

Acknowledgements

I would like to thank Angela Lewis for editing the manuscript - her
feedback and help have been invaluable. Also all the people I
contacted and refer to in the book; I sincerely thank them all for their
co-operation in granting permission to quote extracts from their work,
their research and their artwork.

Also by Marie Louise Lacy

KNOW YOURSELF THROUGH COLOUR

We all love colour, but still so few people realise how colour can change the environment and our lives.

By using some of the simple and effective methods introduced in this book you will discover the power of the colour rays.

Leading scientists are already researching into how and why light/colour has such a profound effect upon all life forms. As we go into the next century people will begin to realise that we are immersed in a light source that feeds and sustains all life. We have only to tune into it to bring healing and harmony into our lives. I hope this book will help you towards discovering this power for yourself.

Foreword

Whilst travelling along the road of personal development, many of us have found Marie Louise Lacy to be an inspiring teacher and guide. I have been privileged to work with her and to be one of her students; knowing her and learning from her has enriched my life.

In 'The Power of Colour to Heal the Environment' Marie Louise embarks upon an exacting task. The subject is broad; its matter is still evolving and changing. She brings together her own deep knowledge and love of her subject, her study and interpretation of the work of Master Omraam Mikhaël Aïvanhov and the work of many pioneers in the use of light and colour. She combines these with her own experience and findings in this field and the result is a multi-faceted, new perspective on how the use of colour and light can really make a positive difference to the world in which we live.

This book has a wide appeal; it contains much that will interest parents, teachers, home-makers and psychologists; those who are in health care, sports and leisure, running businesses or working in law. It contains valuable insights for interior and lighting designers, architects and, of course, colour therapy students and practitioners. And its content, style and presentation will attract those who are simply interested in finding out more about how colour and light affect our lives.

To all who read, I say - you will not be disappointed. Read on, learn and enjoy. There is much to be discovered - and you will take from this book what you yourself need. And as Marie Louise herself will say; "I leave it with you."

Angela Lewis

Editor

Picture credits

Contents

Chapter1: Introduction

Why and how does colour affect our lives?

Colour can transform, uplift and change an atmosphere; we all respond to colour, and today we can bring colour into every part of our lives using materials, fabrics and paints. Since the introduction of chemicals we can dye most things to any colour we require. The colours we like are extensions of ourselves, for around everyone is an aura of light which emits many colours. We tend to be drawn toward those colours which complement our own personal aura.

Our use of language shows how deeply colour forms part of our everyday lives and we use phrases without thinking, such as: "I feel blue", "feeling off colour", "the yellow coward", "green with envy" and so on. We may refer to someone we meet as a "colourful character" and we often notice which colours particularly suit those around us. A simple understanding of the psychology of colour and its deeper significance can bring us harmony, peace and joy and can change our lives beyond measure.

The knowledge of colour has been handed down throughout the ages, observed by many with secondsight, felt by others. The discoveries have led us to understand that the introduction of colour or colours into the environment can change the approach, attitudes and outlook of the people near to those colours; colour can calm, reduce stress and violence, or introduce vitality and energy. Today, qualified colour therapists are using colour in many different ways, for colour therapy is a form of energy medicine. When the right colour is introduced, balance and harmony are gradually restored.

The colours of nature feed us constantly, whether or not we are aware of this. Many scientists now agree that all matter is made from light particles; light is energy and energy is colour. Look through a prism and you will see seven colours; red, orange and yellow (known as the warm colours); blue, indigo and violet (the cool colours) and green (neither warm nor cool). If we include all the shades and tints, these colours together make up thousands of different colourings. New tones are constantly being introduced so we now have a delightfully wide choice from which to choose; yet it is not so long ago that only the wealthy could afford to have lovely colours around them.

Many people do not realise the power of colour. Too many colours, busy patterns and designs can, for example, create a disharmonious environment, and our environment reflects our inner feelings and our outlook. This earth is going through a tremendous transformation; looking back 100 years we can see how enormously technology has advanced, but bringing with it an imbalance within humanity.

Many people are seeking a more simple life, searching for a deeper meaning and purpose. Wherever you go today you will hear people saying they feel stressed, they cannot cope, perhaps saying "I haven't a moment to breathe"... When the true understanding of colour psychology is wider known it can be used in the environment to reduce stress, one of the major factors of ill health today. According to Carlton Wagner, director of the Wagner Institute for Color Research in Santa Barbara, California, the impact of colour can be tremendous although this impact is one of which we are largely unaware. He shows that viewing certain colours actually evokes physical change in us. His findings are joined by those of David Rainey, Ph. D., of John Carroll University in Ohio, who has recently reported such an example; that seeing red stimulates the glandular system and increases the heart rate, blood pressure and respiration. Research has shown that when a person likes a colour his whole system is relaxed. His viewpoint changes and he becomes more optimistic - he sees life differently.

Scientists are finding it is possible to change the molecular structure of all biochemical substances in plants, animals and humans by subjecting them to the colours. When we introduce colours into our environment we change the electromagnetic fields around us. It is also important that we use more natural fibres such as silk, cotton, linen and wool in our clothing and surroundings. Even when we add colour to each of these fibres it retains the vibrational quality unique to itself. It is interesting to note that silk holds the vibration of colour more than any other material; therefore it is often used in a colour therapy treatment.

In 1993, I visited the Institute of HeartMath (I.H.M.) at Boulder Creek, California, and found scientists and sensitives working together studying the DNA and the electro-magnetic fields of energy in which we are immersed. They are pioneering research into the ways of boosting these energy fields. Research at I.H.M. laboratories has shown that negative emotions tax the heart and immune system, whilst positive emotions such as care, appreciation and love increase the efficiency of the heart and boost the immune system. They have discovered that the heart's electrical system is similar to that of a radio transmitter; for it to work properly it must be tuned in to a proper frequency. When there is a frequency distortion, both the heart and the immune system are affected and since the heart's electrical signal is so strong, these frequencies are radiated throughout the entire body and permeate every cell. HeartMath have now introduced self management techniques to transform negative attitudes into positive attitudes and they have found that, as mental and emotional balance is acquired, the brain becomes more efficient, responding by transmitting more peaceful vibrations which in turn encourages more creativity and heightened intuition.

Our attitudes and outlook on life are seen as different colours in the aura. This aura of light surrounds all form, and clairvoyants call it the "Rainbow of Light". When we feel well, we radiate with colour, and when we are unwell these colours appear drab (we even say we feel 'off colour'). As a colour therapist I am aware that colour affects us all at every level of our being, physically, emotionally and mentally; it will become one of the major therapies of the 21st century. We need to harness this tremendous energy in order to improve our lives.

Technology has so speeded up our lives that it is as though we are running after ourselves, always with so much to do. What we need to remember is that we are part of nature; there is a time to work and to play, to rest and to reflect. Much of life today is out of balance and even nature is reacting to the imbalance we have created. Too much stimulating activity upsets the nervous system, yet such activity is widespread. Introducing and using certain colours in our environment can start to bring back a balance into our lives which is currently sadly lacking.

Television, radio and magazines give us many ideas on decor and how to use colour, and some of these are very helpful. However, we need to simplify our approach. Light, which contains all the colours feeds, nourishes and sustains all life and it is how we use this light, and how we apply it to our lives, which will make the difference that is so necessary today.

Chapter 2: Colour Psychology

We all have our colour preferences which change along with our feelings and attitudes. When we love a colour, we tend to inhale and go "ahh" as though drinking it in, whilst colours we do not like can make us feel uncomfortable and sometimes even sickly or unwell. Watch how you react next time you see a colour that you love or do not like; it will tell you quite a lot about yourself. Sometimes you'll find you do not like a colour for reasons you cannot explain; there will be nothing the matter with the colour itself, but its effect on you may be profound. Perhaps, for example, as a child you were held against your will in a room painted the colour in question; such an association may have stayed with you, going deep into the unconscious. The colours we like can change over the years and those you chose when you were younger may not appeal to you now. This is because the colour in your own auric field will have changed, and now attract other colours; observe yourself and give this some thought.

A few years ago I was working in Canada. A television programme about the power of colour was presented, showing how people reacted to different colours. The producers had identically furnished six rooms but had painted each one in a different colour. They installed a hidden camera into each room to observe those taking part in the experiment.

In the red room hardly anyone spoke. They all moved quickly as though in a hurry; some of them said they liked the colour but would not want too much of it in their home. They found it made them restless and agitated and some of them found it disturbing. Quite a few people walked in and immediately walked out again; it was too much for them, and they felt overpowered.

Then they walked into the orange room. Most people started to talk to each other and to discuss whether or not they liked the room. Many became animated and very expressive. Several felt that the orange was too powerful - but some really loved it. They said the colour made them feel warm and they could sense that they would soon have more vitality in a room containing some of this colour.

In the yellow room some sat down to have a proper conversation, not only about the yellow colour but also their reaction to the other colours. They said it reminded them of the sunshine; they had never realised that yellow was such a strong and powerful colour and they were surprised they were reacting so strongly.

When they walked into the green room you could see the relief on all the participants' faces on entering a calmer environment! Some people sat down, some put their feet up and unfolded their arms (always a sign of relaxing). The conversation was softer than in the orange or yellow rooms; it was as though the people present preferred to absorb the colour rather than talk about it. They found it restful and calming, but several people said they did not like green.

In the blue room, everyone spoke softly and moved slowly. Some said it gave them a feeling of peace and tranquillity - others suddenly felt sad and found it disquieting, but they all agreed that blue made them feel cold and they did not wish to stay in the room for too long.

In the violet room it was easily discernible by the participants' expressions that some loved it and others found it most uncomfortable; those who loved it said they could have stayed in the room for ages, whilst some people could not get out of this room quickly enough. Violet penetrates the depths of our being and it can have a religious overtone. It has a fast vibration and induces stillness; many find this disquieting. Those people who stayed in the room longer felt inspired, uplifted and soothed. They felt as though they were in a safe cocoon.

Several people I spoke to after the programme were amazed at the reactions they had witnessed; they had not realised that colour was so powerful and said that in future they would start to notice how colours affected them individually. It has been noted that sixty percent of an individual's reaction to any situation is based on colour (surroundings, clothes etc); so from this we can recognise the importance of having the right colours in our environment, whether at home or at work.

As you will see, our reaction to colour varies; we all have preferences for certain colours and colourings and love wearing and having those colours around us. It is the colours we do not like which tell us a lot about ourselves. For example, when red seems too powerful for us we may have been brought up by a powerful parent. Those of you who are shy, lacking in confidence and needing to express yourselves more need orange. Those of you who do not like yellow do not feel good about yourself; likewise green reminds us of events we would perhaps like to forget. Blue can bring forward sad memories from the past; that is why some people felt sad in the blue room. Violet is a very powerful colour - if you are afraid of power you will not like it, but do remember that it is the way we use our power that is important.

The above is only a very brief overview of how the colours affect us in different ways. In my other book I go into detail about the individual colours, how and why they affect us and how we can introduce them into our lives (Know Yourself Through Colour).

The influence of each colour

Red

When this colour is seen through a prism it is a beautiful scarlet, a very powerful colour. It makes us feel adventurous, daring, powerful and courageous. We all need some red in our aura to help us to be motivated. Red is a pioneering colour that seeks attention; the tints and shades bring many qualities, from inducing caring for others to being ruthless and only thinking about oneself. There is a tendency to dominate others, and this is why the colour needs golden yellow (which is wisdom) or green to act as a balance. Blue will cool the red colour from going to extremes. True scarlet makes us vibrant and to realise we can do anything once we make up our minds.

This colour affects our emotional responses - and not always for the better! When dark shades of red are introduced into the environment they can activate people to violence within; red excites our basic tendencies and stimulates action before thought. Red can stimulate appetite and it is possible to lose track of time when surrounded with this colour; theatres, fast food restaurants bars and casinos may deliberately be decorated in red for this reason.

Darker reds sometimes bring out our darker side; for example, we refer to "red light districts" where sex can be purchased. From a psychological viewpoint this shade denotes ruthlessness and it can activate violence within people, but usually only when the environment contains a lot of the colour.

When used sparingly it has a more positive effect and when complemented with green a balance is brought to the powerful red energy.

Pink Colours

Pink is created when white is blended with red; the many different shades of pink depend on the amount of white used. Rose pink gives warmth; paler pinks may be relaxing but even though we have become used to using very pale pinks in our decor we should know that these shades can have a draining effect. Warmer pinks have a positive effect and under their influence people become active, wanting to get on. Surround older people, perhaps living on their own, with pale colours and they will often become listless and disinterested in life - the introduction of some warmer pink tones will create a personality change and those who have formerly felt drained of energy will become active and energetic members of society.

Orange

This colour can be too powerful for most people, but when introduced in the paler tints of peach and orange they like it. A faster vibration than red, orange encourages us to wake up to our inner potential, stand up for ourselves and be more confident. Conditioning as a child can often inhibit us. Let us make our dreams come true, communicate our inner feelings and express them. This colour stimulates conversation, and is the colour of vitality, creativity and warmth.

The paler orange colours relax us and we become more of our true self. We find we are able to communicate more and for many, the surprise that they have a desire to use their creativity if they are not doing so already. Several years ago I met a lady who had just moved into a new house. There were orange cupboards in the kitchen which she did not like, but which she could not afford to change. Her husband had taken a new job which involved a lot of entertaining and, although she had never before liked cooking, to her amazement she found herself actually enjoying trying out new recipes. Her friends complimented her and today she is a good cook. How often we wish we could do something, and yet never get started! Well, the orange energy helps us; we should surround ourselves with an orange colouring that we like and it will stimulate our creative powers. Always remember, though, to have another colour to complement it; in this case you could use green for the walls.

The orange colour is also used by fast food restaurants as they know it creates a friendly atmosphere in which children are welcome. As the colour has a lot of vitality within it customers do not stay too long, so it induces a quick turnover!

Dark Orange

Whereas clear orange vivifies and brings us to life the darker oranges can have a negative, more sedative effect. Mix black with orange and it becomes brown, a colour which in nature is wonderful but should be avoided in decor unless it is the hue of a natural material (See section on Brown).

Dark orange can create a depressive atmosphere and should never be used in decor. It also creates a feeling of helplessness and inadequacy.

Paler Orange

A colour that gives a feeling of warmth, joy and free expression. Introduce this colour into the home or the workplace and you will begin to feel good about yourself - the energy of orange expands the aura so, as long as you have a clear idea of what you wish to achieve, the colour will give you the energy to go forward and succeed. All creative artists love using this colour, especially with blue, which complements it well.

Yellow

This colour is associated with sunlight and it feels as though it has no boundaries. Yellow is a warm and expansive colour which activates the mind and opens us up to new ideas. People who feel good about themselves usually love the colour. It enhances our awareness and we become more alert; this vibration also helps those with learning difficulties. Yellow affects the solar plexus - the heart of the central nervous system and a major centre within us that feeds the brain with information.   It is through the solar plexus that we sense whether something is right or wrong.

Yellow boosts the ego, and can stimulate the deepest recesses of the mind and bring clarity. When a person has too much yellow in the aura they can be conceited - and we call them egocentric. But we all need some of the colour vibration; it helps us to receive knowledge and increases our awareness of a greater reality. It has been known for objects to disappear in a room which is predominantly yellow; it tends to make people lose their sense of limitation and things can go missing. They lose their sense of boundaries; what is theirs and what is not theirs. When used with blue the colour is balanced. Always remember that yellow and white together can overstimulate the mind, perhaps creating slight instability and insecurity, and so should be used with discretion and together with other colours to bring balance. Used in hallways, corridors and places where there is very little light, yellow can create a feeling of space. In a cottage with oak beams the contrast between the natural wood and yellow is most effective, but another colour - such as rose pink or blue - should always be used to balance the yellow energy.

Golden Yellow

When you introduce this colour with its warm overtones make sure you complement it with a brighter colour. Where there is a lot of light this colour radiates; it can be used in conservatories, and light hallways. It gives a feeling of luxury that is difficult to define.

Darker Yellows

These colours can have an adverse effect upon us. It is the energy which creates pessimism and negativity toward others, and is the colour associated with the aura of the "yellow coward." Dark yellows can make us feel unwell and reflect badly on the complexion, as we appear yellow and sapped of energy. It is wise not to wear mustard and acid yellows for this reason as they only negate our energy. Mustard yellow is also associated with deviousness.

Paler Yellows

Some pale yellows give a feeling of space and a mental lift; too pale a colour can also sap energy. Think of the sun which, in its palest wintry shades, does not have its usual vibrant luminosity.

Green

The colour of balance and harmony, when we look through a prism green is in the middle of the spectrum. Neither warm nor cold, it goes with all the other colours and helps to reduce tension and stress.

Green is a colour that links with our self esteem. Known to reduce blood pressure it can affect some people emotionally if they have unresolved issues; this is why not everyone likes green, but it is a colour that lifts our vibrations and helps us to flow with events. Green creates the feeling you have when you go out for a walk in the woods and fields; a profound sense of freedom and letting go. This colour is relaxing and restful - but never use it on its own, as it can be draining and can create a static environment. In business it should be used sparingly; it is not a power colour, but in the home with a warm peach or rose pink it will create a soothing, relaxing atmosphere.

Darker Greens

These colours bring a sense of strength and stability but should only be used in larger establishments and with paler colours.

Paler Greens

These colours help us to feel good about ourselves; children love pale green tones as they are close to nature and still feel its presence. Adults have usually lost the feeling of oneness with their environment as a result of conditioning education and we all need to rediscover that state of wonderment at all creation, the awareness that everything around us is alive and emits energy. Green affects the heart centre and encourages us to be more caring.

Blue

Most people love blue. It is known to be a very healing colour; soothing, calming and cooling. Depending on the blue we associate it with loyalty, integrity, respect, responsibility and authority. Some blue colourings help to reduce violence - and graffiti - in the environment. We have only to look up into the sky and its immensity to feel a reverence for life and for all that is beautiful and sacred.

Like all colours, there are many tints and shades radiating a different energy and affecting us in different ways. It will depend on the environment as to which colour you choose. Blue is very effective in hospitals and clinics but it needs to be used with care and insight, otherwise it can create a cold environment. Always use a warm colour to go with it. Too much blue will make a person become aloof and withdrawn - but blue helps to lower blood pressure and reduce stress and tension; it can also make us feel sleepy.

Deep Blues

The use of royal blue can be very effective - and can have a deep effect upon us. It does not have its name for nothing! Royal blue brings out the very best in people; those who cheat, lie or who are underhand will find, when surrounded with this colour, that they begin to feel guilty and start to change their behaviour. It is a good colour to use for some of our institutions; its energy tends to bring out loyality, integrity and honesty, all of which are attributes of this colour. Use it with any warm colour; its fast vibration will affect that colour, too.

When used with yellow, royal blue activates the mind and the intuition. Used with red it brings out emotion, strengthening our opinions. With rose pink it brings out the caring side of our natures. Royal blue and peach encourages creativity; royal blue and orange increases communication skills and encourages a true responsibility - be true to yourself and do what you feel you want to, and not what you feel you have to! All those working within the media would be helped by this colour combination, which would bring out only the best within them to impart to the public. Royal blue energy clears out the dross and releases clearer perceptions. I would not suggest its use for walls but it can be used to paint doors, window frames and skirting boards, or perhaps as the colour for a picture frame.

Indigo

During an experiment some years ago, a room within a clinic was painted indigo with a white ceiling. It was to be used as a rest room for visiting doctors and therapists and was created to see how they would react. Many found that they fell asleep when they had been sitting in the room for a short while; a few felt fearful and others found they could not bear to be in the room at all. Indigo can have this effect upon us; although it is a colour in its own right it looks nearly black, and it touches our deep inner emotions and thoughts. Its vibration is very powerful. In colour therapy it is used to bring out old fears - pink helps to release them. It may be interesting to note that the therapists' rest room colour has now been changed!

Paler Blue

Use this colour with warm pinks or orange colours, for on its own or with white it can create a feeling of coldness and often leads to introspection.

Violet

Not everyone likes violet; but those who do love it! This colour has a very fast vibration and it encourages us to reach higher in our creativity of music and the arts to give the best of ourselves in all that we undertake. Violet is associated with high ideals, devotion and loyalty to a cause, which might include some form of sacrifice. Many great artists and musicians have used it as inspiration. Like all colours, there are many shades from which to choose, each of which has its own effect; in large rooms and entrance halls it imparts a feeling of grandeur. When used with yellow, its complementary colour, it encourages us to go within to find our innermost being which we all have and which so few of us use; the yellow stimulates the mind in this process. Used with green, violet inspires us to help others, on a local or far grander international scale. This is because green is associated with our higher emotions and, depending on the shade of green used, can motivate us in different ways. Violet with a paler green encourages us to be more caring whereas the darker greens as seen in nature give us strength and would go well with a paler violet. You can use violet and yellow for a theatre. Introduce violet for curtains, chairs and the theatre boxes - not interiors - and have a pale gold yellow for the walls; green can also be used to balance these two colours. The violet will create an atmosphere of reverent expectancy.

Of all the colours, violet is the most powerful, and utmost care is needed as to where and how it is used. Use of red and violet together would overpower most people; even when there is some green in the decor. It is very rare to see these two colours used together but it would indicate someone who is very creative and good at what they do (violet) and want others to know about it (red). If living in an environment with these two colours do use green as well - otherwise you will become unbalanced.

(see chart of complementary colours).

Purple

This colour can be used in a setting where there are a lot of beautiful things, and should always be used with green. Purple contains quite a lot of red and this activates our basic feelings, so we may become quite emotional and react accordingly.

Paler Violet

An ethereal colour, pale violet can be used with other colours but should not be used as the main colour for a room. It creates a lack of grounding and, in time, a person would become disinterested in the surrounding world.

Magenta

This colour contains both red and violet and is very uplifting. It is rich and dramatic and looks good in the home, especially in large establishments. I recently visited an hotel which featured this colour in its chairs, with greens and pinks as a background. The combination was not only effective - it gave a feeling of luxury and a place in which clientele are cared for. I later gathered from the friends who took me there that this is, in fact, true.

If you want to lift the vibrations of your business, then introduce some of this colour into the decor; it can inspire people and encourage them to take initiative. Magenta goes well with green - these two colours enhance each other.

Turquoise

This is a very relaxing and soothing colour but should always be used in conjunction with a warm colour to ensure balance. As the main colour of the decorative theme it looks wonderful, and it does help to quickly reduce stress. Turquoise contains blue and green, both of which are calming colours in their own right. Decorate a lecture hall in this colour combined with white and including the warmer tones of, say, pink or peach for chairs and you will create an atmosphere of restfulness combined with openness to the speaker, or to whatever activity is taking place there. In colour therapy turquoise is used as a most effective aid to calming the nervous system.

Brown

This colour gives the feeling of everything permanent, solid and secure. In the last century brown was used regularly and it contributed to man becoming rather fixed in his ideas and approach. In today's age we have to be flexible; make sure brown does not hold you back from going forward. Brown is the colour of stability and when used in its natural state, as in floors and furniture, it emits an energy conducive to our surroundings.

Yellow in combination with brown can give it more energy; otherwise use it sparingly. It is interesting to note that a lot of brown can usually be found in rented accommodation such as flats, bedsits etc. - a subtle indication of the holding energy of this colour.

Grey

This colour has proved popular with interior designers - largely because of its potential for co-ordination. When you choose to use it with other colours it can look effective. But grey is associated with fear and I feel there is enough negativity in this world at present - we do not need to create more. Therefore my suggestion is that if you decide to use grey, use it sparingly, in its palest shades, and use it in combination with colours which will have a balancing, positive effect, such as red, orange and yellow tones.

White

White enhances all the colours. I once came upon a totally white room at an exhibition. Although it was most effective, to me it lacked the character and the depth which the introduction of colour creates. All white walls look marvellous (at least, if you have no children!) and allow you to introduce colour into the curtains, flooring and accessories; the effect can be stunning and most dramatic, and the colours you choose will take on a startling radiance and luminosity.

Black

Black is power - but only when used with another colour. It can otherwise make us seem aloof; unapproachable and intimidating to the extreme. In time to come we shall not use black in our decor at all. We, as human beings, need the light rays to nourish and feed us; to help us find our true potential to grow and then we will develop in amazing ways.

Mixing the colours

To create a colour, we blend together two primaries. To create a variety of different and subtle effects, we can use two or more different colours together simultaneously. When using colour in this way understand the basic rule; the largest amount of colour conveys the strongest message.

And when using contrasting colours together with a neutral colour you will elicit the reactions to both colours.

Lighter colours do not always project the essence of the original colour. For example, whilst red excites, certain pinks bring a soothing energy. In the same way, a colour made by mixing two primaries does not retain the properties of these original primaries; it instead has its own distinct energy.

For example, yellow is power whilst red is exciting and demands attention; when mixed together, they create orange, which is openness, friendliness and is the energy of communication. So orange takes some of the properties of yellow and red but expresses them in a very different way.

We tend to classify colours as "bright", "pale" and "rich". Each has its own energy wavelength and, for example, colours such as magenta, deep greens and burgundy are often found in rich, stately homes or large establishments, as they lend themselves to these kinds of environments. It is important to always remember that colour creates the mood and the feeling of any environment.

The Colour Circle

Colours opposite to each other on the circle are described as 'complementary' (see diagram on page 28).

Red is opposite Green

Orange is opposite Blue

Yellow is opposite Violet

Salmon is opposite Turquoise

Golden Yellow is opposite Purple

Lime is opposite Magenta

All these colours complement and enhance each other, but never use them as strong colours together except on very rare occasions. People would find them too powerful. Choose one of the colours as your main colour - and then complement it with a paler tint of its complementary colour.

Other colour combinations which go together using their shades and tints

Red and Blue

Orange and Turquoise

Yellow and Blue

Orange and Green

Green and Violet

Magenta and Green or Blue

THE KEY is always to introduce a warm and a cool colour and use them together. Our world is a world of duality; day and night, hot and cold, joy and sadness etc. Electricity has two poles, the positive and the negative. The same principle runs throughout creation, bringing a balance as in nature - the use of colour is no exception to this rule (See 'Colour Circle').

THE COLOUR CIRCLE
Complementary Colours

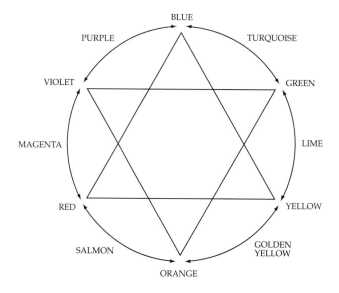

Cold electrical colours are above:
Warm magnetic colours are below

COMPLEMENTARY COLOURS
as seen in the Colour Circle

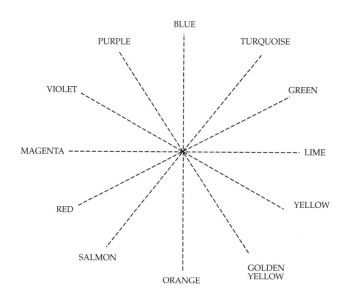

Chapter 3: Colour in the Home

The colours we use in our homes say a lot about us and here we shall undertake an exploration of the rooms in the home, looking at the implications and the effects of many of the colours which may be found there.

The Hall

As we enter a person's home our first impression is the one we remember. Colour is a language and gives out signals about ourselves - it makes statements about us. We usually react to colour unconsciously, but are aware of how we feel.

Let's take a look at some of the colour choices for halls and their likely psychological effects.

A yellow entrance hall usually indicates a person who has ideas and a wide field of interests. A home belonging to an academic would probably contain a distinctive shade of yellow as this colour is associated with the intellect, ideas and a searching mind.

On the other hand a green entrance hall - say, a warm, apple green - indicates a home in which children, family and pets are held in high importance; those who love green also tend to hoard possessions and never throw anything away, so the rest of the home may be a little busy! Green used with paler colours gives an energy of relaxation and peace. Not everyone likes this colour; it affects our deepest inner feelings. For example, those who tend to hold on to deep resentments and feel very hurt inside find this colour difficult to deal with. It is also connected with our self esteem, as to whether we think highly or have a low opinion of ourselves.

A warm pink entrance hall indicates a home which is warm and loving.   People using this colour like to care for others - but can sometimes be possessive, particularly with their family.

A blue entrance hall indicates a place in which people have strong opinions - there could be a tendency to appear aloof, as they can be absorbed too much in their own world. They are often loners but kind and thoughtful, independent and usually self sufficient.

When mainly red is used for the entrance hall it would indicate a person who likes to be noticed; often the pioneer, who will be very restless if they do not channel their energies into something constructive. When they do so they are very active within their environment.

Perhaps your hall is, at this present time, a shade of cream. You can bring in other colours by introducing pictures or ornaments - if there is a window, then choose a colourful curtain. For many years cream has been used in the home because it is "safe" - however, it is a very neutral colour and, although there is nothing wrong with it, it imparts very little energy. Used in combination with other tones it can provide a canvass for your experiments with colour.

The Kitchen

The room where food is prepared is one of the most important in the home. How you feel when you are preparing food will affect both you and those who eat with you, and a lot of thought needs to go not only into the kitchen's practical design, but also into its colours. You may not be able to change the colours of the cupboards; but the rest of the kitchen decor can be changed. Since our attitude whilst we do anything affects the ensuing result, use of the right colours in the kitchen is of extreme importance. As time goes on we shall become more and more aware of how our thoughts and feelings influence what we do; so it is important to choose colours which will help us with our activities.

So often today the kitchen is the centre of the home; the family congregates here to eat, talk and to relax. Therefore we need to create an environment which is conducive to feeling relaxed and happy.

Blue colours are inadvisable; they will only tend to separate the family, since we respond to blue by becoming withdrawn, and keeping any disturbed feelings to ourselves. But introduce warm pink or peach as the main colour and the family will be drawn closer together, encouraged to share their feelings and differences and discuss these more easily. Pink helps us to relax, let go, unwind and feel at ease; it releases stress and tension and looks well with green or blue as its complementary colour. But it is important to use a warm pink - kitchens should feature a warm shade as the main colour.

There is one important exception to this rule; although red is a warm colour, use sparingly in the kitchen. It can activate negative feelings and, as it is such an emotional colour, arouses us very quickly. It is particularly important to keep away from red if you know you have a quick temper!

Orange, peach and apricot are very creative colours and will tend to activate your innate creativity. For instance, you will find yourself becoming more interested in how to prepare and present food attractively for yourself and your family . These colours generally induce a greater interest in the home.

Yellow is usually a bright colour depending on the shade or tint chosen; but the effects of yellow are not relaxing. Under its influence we tend to eat our meals more quickly and talk a lot whilst we eat, which does not aid our digestion - it is quite the opposite to the desired atmosphere of warmth and relaxation in the kitchen.

The Dining Room

Today this room has fallen almost into disuse unless we are entertaining. As you now know, we create atmospheres by using different colours to which people respond accordingly. If the aim is to enjoy stimulating conversation in the dining room, choose a bright (but not acid) yellow or one of the orange shades as your main colour to encourage conviviality and sociability. Choose blue for a dining room and the conversation will tend to be about more serious issues, perhaps politics, business or world issues. Within a yellow environment these issues will still be discussed but the yellow will activate the ego of each person present, so all will be wanting to have their say rather than listening to the views of others around the table. When red colours are used in the dining room they will create an intimate feeling and the conversation will tend to be more personal.

Here I have focussed on the main colour and its effects; always use a complementary colour (or other enhancing tones) together with the main colour to provide a pleasing effect.

The Bedroom

Here, our choice of colour needs to be cooling and calming - we will then become rested before going to sleep. Blue colourings release the pressure from our day's activities. Choosing one of the cooler colours will immediately "cool" the activity of the brain cells, helping to slow the incessant chatter of the mind. The body recharges itself whilst we are asleep. If the room is decorated with a mixture of bright colours these will continue to stimulate the nervous system whilst we slumber - therefore although we think we have had a good night's rest, the body has not been able truly to relax. It is also important to avoid using too many patterns.

A lady I met years ago told me that she had decorated her bedroom in red and white. When I said these colours are over-stimulating, she became angry and totally disagreed. She did not choose to stay around to even hear my explanation of how these colours over-energise! Her behaviour was typical of someone on overdrive and hyperactive, and underlined the very point I was making about red; she was absorbing so much of the red energy that it was affecting her personality.

Do remember that when you are asleep you absorb energy more quickly - so the colours you choose for your bedroom will strongly affect you. Do not put up with colours which displease you, thinking it does not matter and you will get around to decorating the room some time; it matters very much,

and your displeasure is an important message to which you should listen. This is a regular experience for people moving house; my advice is always 'decorate the bedrooms first!'

Colour co-ordinated suggestions for bedrooms:- turquoise, made up from green and blue, which calms the emotions and helps us to relax. It is not as cold a colour as blue but both go well with peach, pink or salmon colours.

Do avoid yellow tones as the main colour for a bedroom; even a pale yellow will overstimulate the mind. It may look very pretty, but it will still affect you at the mental level, so if you love yellow think about other rooms in your home in which it can safely be used. Pale apple green with a warm colour go well together but choose the pink colour for the walls and use both colours for the accessories.

Children's Bedrooms

There is such a wide, interesting and tempting choice for a child's room today that it may seem overwhelming to try to choose. But I have a strong and important message which I hope will influence your choice; *keep it simple!* The information about the effects of busy choices discussed in the previous 'bedroom' paragraphs cannot be overemphasised when it comes to children. Too many colours and patterns will over-energise a child. During the day most children's minds are overstimulated in any case, and their minds are constantly buzzing with all they have seen and heard. To provide a restful, calming environment for their sleep choose pale colours for the walls and introduce some brighter colours in the furnishings. Pink or peach lampshades are best; do not use blue or green, because these colours will have a disturbing effect (see chapter on lighting).

All children tend to have vivid imaginations. The introduction of patterns - stripes and particularly stars - to the ceiling will disturb and upset some children. The more peaceful the room and atmosphere created, the more happy will be the child. A ceiling of pale blue will help the child to have more restful sleep; waking in the middle of the night to see this will have a calming and soothing effect.

The Nursery - a Baby's Room

Until the age of 18 months a baby usually has a very delicate aura. Strong colours in the room of such an infant will overstimulate and overactivate. Brighter colours should only be used after this first period, once the brain development is complete. For the first eighteen months use pale pinks and blues; and remember the pale blue ceiling recommended for children's rooms. Should the mother have experienced a difficult pregnancy use pink for the walls; this is the colour of love and warmth. Many people today may not realise that the child in the womb is affected by the mother's emotions, mental attitude and the surrounding environment. The child needs to feel wanted and loved, but under difficult circumstances the mother may offer only rejection.   A pink room will help both mother and baby, surrounding both with the warmth of love; the more these feelings are experienced, the more content will be the child.

You can see why it is so very important to choose the right colours for the nursery - their influence can be very helpful. During the first, formative years of a child's life its brain is absorbent as a sponge - how vital, then, to ensure that the colours chosen have a positive effect.

The Bathroom

Pink and peach colours give the body a warm glow and we quickly let go of tension and relax in such an atmosphere. Yellow can inspire us to have ideas as we soak and blue will certainly calm and cool us down - although we would not linger long in a blue bathroom unless very tired. The blue colour should be avoided for those who become easily depressed; if it cannot be changed it should be complemented by warm colours on the walls and co-ordinating towels. There is a wonderful saying "Think Pink." When you feel low or depressed, this colour will lift your spirits and help you to feel good about yourself. Avoid black and dark colours in a bathroom; mirrors will make the bathroom seem larger and reflect back other colours. Introducing plants into the room also brings in the life force energy (but first find out which plants like the steamy atmosphere).

Flats and Maisonettes

The entrance hall to a block of flats is a most important area. The hall should be bright, cheerful and blend where possible with the theme of the exterior paintwork - shutters, window frames and so on. Use only three colours for the overall theme - white is counted as a colour - and apply the same rule to maisonettes. Yellow is a good colour to use for a bright hallway; it makes the area seem bigger than it really is. Using the same coloured carpet throughout will give a feeling of spaciousness but avoid too many patterns, otherwise you will make the atmosphere too busy, and this will affect your aura. This does not mean you cannot introduce patterns; but either have the carpets or your curtains plain, and complement them with a pattern which combines the colours you have introduced into your home. The result will be far more effective and restful.

Bedsits

So often lack of colour is the feature of the bedsit! Known as "one roomed flatlets", thousands of people live in this type of dwelling, usually in towns and cities and usually furnished in drab and colourless fashion by the landlord. No wonder people feel stressed in such an environment! They get up, go to work, come home, quite often watch the television and then go to bed. I am, of course, exaggerating; not all live this kind of life, but its echoes can be felt in bedsit land and it is often a struggle to keep going. What a world of difference the use of colour can make! To paint a room in lovely colours and to complement these with cheerful furnishings provides a tonic which is difficult to equal, and results in quite a different approach to life.

Very many of these dwellings seem to have beige walls, brown carpets and mustard yellow or dark orange curtains. Introducing pink or peach, either in the walls or in the furnishings and complementing this with some green or blue tones would have a profoundly positive effect upon the inmates. There would be an altogether greater enthusiasm about life which would take on a completely different meaning.

So landlords have a huge responsibility! As well as providing a home fit to inhabit, the provision of a cheerfully decorated home results in happier, less stressed inhabitants who will be more willing to co-operate and take pride in their homes should any work need to be done. Sadly, for many at present home is just a place to sleep and circumstances seem to dictate the acceptance of a dismal atmosphere. To those landlords who have introduced some lovely colours into their bedsits I say 'Congratulations! Let us hope others will follow your example.'

Clearing Your Home

We all collect so much clutter in our homes that from time to time we need to have a good clear out. Everything holds energy, and when we admire or use an object its energy remains alive. If the object falls into disuse or is disliked it can radiate a negative energy; both energy fields have an effect upon us. Moving home can be good for us; at this time we tend to be ruthless and rid ourselves of items we have not used for some time. Clearing out in this way makes room for new energy to enter our lives. Start by ridding yourself of old books you no longer require; pass on unused cassettes to other people who may want them and clear out ornaments, old clothes and any items you do not use any more. You will be so surprised at the difference this will make! Second hand furniture holds the vibrations of those who used it before you, so be careful what you buy. Someone I once knew had a lovely saying: " If your glass is full, you cannot put any more into it - so if you want to make changes in your life and to move on within yourself, then have a good clear out!"

Blessing Your Home

When you have moved into another home, make it your own. Always surround it with light. See it bathed in sunlight and clear other people's vibrations by saying a prayer, or by standing in a room and inviting the light (imagine sunlight) into yourself to fill you and the room. I have used this method and it works. No matter how lovely the previous owner of the property seemed to be, be wise; clear and cleanse your home. Ask love, light, joy and peace to be present and bless and give thanks that it is so. Light can be brought into any area to clear negative vibrations. Always ask that the place be blessed for the highest good of all.

Inviting good energies into your home, your work and each of your environments will make a lot of difference to the quality of your life.

Complementary Notes

1. When decorating your home, decide upon three main colours for the whole house and follow the theme with furnishings and accessories. You will still have a wide choice because of the many tints and shades of the colours you have chosen, but you will bring harmony into your home (three is a key number to balance energies; think of the three sides which make a triangle, the corners of which have no stress, whereas the number four makes four sides and the corners are always in a state of stress). See chapter on Form, Shape and Colour.

2. Think along the following lines; predominantly warm colours downstairs, and cooler colours upstairs. If you live on one floor then choose a warm colour for the main tones in your living areas, and a cool colour as your main shade for the bedrooms, and complement each with its appropriate colour. Always remember it is the main colour which will give the strongest effect.

    (refer to the page 28 on complementary colours)

Chapter 4: Colour and Education

Nursery Schools

When children start nursery school for the first time, they leave behind a familiar home environment. They meet adults and other children whom they may not have met before and many find it frightening; it is essential, therefore, that the colour/s used for their rooms feel warm and inviting. Warm rose pinks, peaches and apricots will help to give the safe feeling which is so important to a child. These warm colours will reduce the preconceived fears the child may have as the first steps are taken into a nursery school. A small child will know immediately whether he or she likes the people or the place, and will react instantly. Light greens go well with these warm colours and help to create a calming and relaxing atmosphere. If blue is introduced into the colour scheme care should be taken to ensure it is a bright blue; children of this age love colour and respond very quickly. The toys in the room can be very colourful but should be the clear colours as found in the prism - and not dark shades, for these can be disturbing to the child. The sensitivity of children should never be underestimated, even if they appear to be well balanced, for at this age they are far more aware at some levels than are many adults.

Red and orange are colours that children love and need. Orange is good for those who are shy but also for the extrovert child, because it channels their energies into creativity. As children play, it is always useful to observe which colours they like; it will help in understanding the child better. Should a child be drawn to yellow this would indicate an alert mind. A child liking violet tends to be over sensitive and therefore needing more attention. Children who love blue are quieter and can appear aloof. They need encouragement and the red/orange colours. Those who like red are already the leaders, and can sometimes have a disruptive influence over the other children. Do not use yellow in the decor as this will only make the child feel insecure and spaced out. Yellow has no boundaries and that is so necessary to a young child; they need to feel safe and secure.

If parents and teachers observe the behaviour of children in these early years it will give them insight into how these young people will develop. In terms of development, the first seven years of a child's life are the most important; they lay the foundation stones of the child's character, whereas the temperament of the child is already formed.

Young children usually do not like big rooms, as they need to relate to a place which feels cosy, safe, warm and friendly. In a safe environment they will settle down quickly to enjoy the company of the other children. Encourage those children who seem disturbed and distressed to paint using pink, orange and green colours. This will help them to communicate more and the pink will always open up a child, often helping to release that which is troubling them. If the child continues to be distressed then give him or her something blue to hold - this will have a calming effect.

Schools

Rudolf Steiner introduced an educational system which is still being used today. A scientist, philosopher and teacher, he was well known in the early part of this century for his work. Today, there are several Steiner schools, and they introduce the importance of colour and music as part of the school curriculum. Every student is also taught to play a musical instrument and is encouraged to express his or her individuality. In time to come Steiner's methods will be studied more closely - he was aware that we are multi-faceted beings, and to develop only the intellect brings the imbalance which most people are experiencing today. He advocated that every young child needs red and pink, and introduced this into the form rooms of the first year students. Two young boys of a friend of mine attended a Steiner school and I asked them about the colours - they thought they were "great", and especially liked the pink. The whole room was not decorated in red and pink but, however, these two colours created a feature which acted as a focus. As the students moved up through the school the classrooms were decorated in different colours, from yellow - which helps the intellect and gives us greater awareness and can also help with learning difficulties, but should never be used on its own - to blue which encourages students to use their own perceptions and to think for themselves. Violet was used for those studying music and the arts. The use of green and warm rose pink together is ideal for the rooms of students deciding which subjects to continue to study for their higher exams - the colours will enable them to review what they want to do in life before taking the next step forward.

Whichever the main colour of choice it can be used on the wall behind the teacher's desk as well as being introduced as a feature for the room. In the red/pink room a warm rose pink would be advisable with pale blue ceilings, skirting boards and doors. *(NB. When royal blue paint is used for the doors and skirting boards throughout a school there will be a marked improvement in the behaviour of the students).*

Research Studies Using Colour in Schools

In Canada, Professor Harry Wohlfarth *(see complementary note 1)* and his associate Catherine Sam conducted a series of research studies to see the effects of colour on students at different schools. At one school an all yellow and an all blue room were introduced to see what effect these would have on the students. The rooms had white ceilings. One of the teachers was assigned to the blue room and her comments were very interesting. She immediately felt relaxed, comfortable and found it easy to concentrate for long periods of time without feeling any stress or tension. She found the students settled down quickly, were less impatient, calmer and less excited and their concentration improved; but they were sleepy in the afternoons. The students agreed they were less talkative but felt sleepy in the afternoon. She also noticed that students stopped complaining of headaches and eyestrain.

The next term the same teacher was assigned to the yellow room. The effect was instant; everything seemed hectic and it took longer to become organised. She felt she was less patient with the students' disruptions and at times felt hot and irritable. She usually had a headache but she was less sleepy in the afternoons. The effect on the students was quite marked. They took a long while to settle in class, constantly complained, were loud and boisterous and refused to work. They daily asked for the lights to be turned off because of the glare of the yellow. After several weeks they asked if the room could be painted blue and even offered to paint it themselves. They all found it an instant relief after they had been moved back into the blue room and the teacher found she had better control of the students; but they reverted to feeling sleepy in the afternoons. The overall concensus was that blue is more conducive to learning and more productive; to this, the students also agreed.

Some interesting conclusions arise as a result of these findings. To paint a room all in one colour is too much - but the main colour can be beneficial on one wall behind the teacher, with window frames and doors painted in a pale tint of the same colour ; the rest of the room can then be in a paler complementary colour to introduce a balance. When blue was used in other areas of the school (for example, in the library) the place became quiet, and when used in the washrooms problems became non-existent; for example, production of grafiti virtually stopped.

Research Study in Four Elementary Schools

This study involved four similar elementary schools in Wetaskiwin, Alberta, Canada. Professor Wohlfarth used a warm shade of yellow with light blue wall paint replacing the existing colours of orange, white, beige and brown. He also replaced the cool fluorescent lights with full spectrum lighting. *Different conditions were introduced for each school.* The first school was left with its original colours and lighting so as to observe the contrasts. In the second school both the colours and lighting were changed. In the third school only the lighting was changed and in the fourth school only the colours were changed.

The results were very interesting. In the *first school* there was no change. In the *second school* there was a marked change in students' attitudes and approach and they were less stressed. In the *third school* there was a slight change; full spectrum lighting reduces tiredness and eye strain. In the *fourth school* discipline was better but only the colour had been changed.

This result shows what a difference colour and lighting together made to students in *school two*. Their exam results and IQ tests were also greatly improved; the students were less moody and there was less absenteeism due to ill health. The study was done over a twelve month period ie. a whole school year. By using two colours, one from the warm spectrum and one from the cool spectrum a balance is created that is needed for the psyche. Even in the Rudolf Steiner schools the wisdom of using a complementary colour in a paler tone to act as a balance can be seen. Yellow will always stimulate the intellect, whereas blue will have a calming effect on the mind. Use the colours in balance - two thirds yellow and one third blue - throughout the room, with white, off white or pale blue ceiling and windows. The "black"board could also be a blue colour.

Research Study on the Effects of Colour on Severely Handicapped Children

Studies reveal a distinct difference in behaviour patterns when colour is used.

Staff have to deal with many different situations when dealing with the varied human handicaps. In class many can be aggressive, destructive, self-abusive and often non-attentive, leaving the group activity and completely ignoring the teacher. They can even inflict bodily harm upon themselves.

The research study took place at Elves Memorial Child Development Centre, a school for handicapped children in Edmonton, Alberta, Canada. The object was to study and measure the impact of colour and lighting on the students' behaviour and their physiological patterns in the school environment. It included blind children with severe behaviour disorders, as well as sighted children with severe handicaps.

A room was decorated with a large orange panel on one wall; the other walls were painted off white. Cupboards, shelving etc. were all yellow, the chairs a neutral grey and the tables blue and peach; the floorcovering was orange. The children and staff used the room for ten days, then went home for a holiday, during which time the room was redecorated. Orange was replaced with medium royal blue; cupboards and shelving were also in the same shade of royal blue. Otherwise the furnishings remained the same. The childrens' pulse and blood pressure was consistently taken throughout the whole study.

In the room which was mostly orange, the blood pressure was highest at mid-day and the pulse rates highest in the afternoon. The children were more attentive and the staff were able to vary the activities introduced. When the room had blue as its main colour the students were calmer, quieter and easier to cope with. Their blood pressure was lower and more stable. As the children were easier to handle the staff were far more relaxed and felt better. Blind children also reacted in the same way (studies have shown that blind children pick up the vibrations of the colours).

After 15 days the children were then taken to an environment similar to the first room - mainly orange. To begin with they did not react to the orange in the room, but after a while they responded. Although the physiological measurements showed very little change for the teaching staff they agreed that the children had improved and that it had helped them to relax more and accomplish more in class, particularly in the room with the medium shade of royal blue.

This study took place several years ago and wonderful research has continued. The panel could be made to be reversible, showing the orange colour in the morning and the blue colour for the afternoon. The yellow cupboards and shelving and the rest of the decor to remain the same except the chairs, to be in a pale blue.

Learning Difficulties

Schools and or residential centres specialising in teaching those with learning difficulties would be wise to include orange and blue colourings in their decor. The orange will help to release blocked up emotions within a student and the blue is a very healing colour. Feelings of inadequacy and frustration suppress energy and this can result in an outburst of aggression or anger. Orange tends, under guidance, to channel this energy into a creative activity, at the same time giving the person some vitality.

One has to be careful when using yellow in such circumstances; it is a vibrant colour. Although it is known to stimulate the mind and the nervous system if too much of the colour is used it can bring about extreme tiredness and fatigue. If used always use warm yellows.

Make sure you use the paler tones of orange and the warmer blues - if you do not wish to decorate a whole room you can always try introducing the colours by using materials instead; use either cotton or silk, not synthetics. This will be an effective way to give you a good idea of how the students will respond to these different colourings.

For those of you who work with mentally handicapped people, please note that colour can make a major difference. *However, clear and expert advice is needed to create the maximum beneficial effect.* I do think the time is now long overdue to research into these methods, certainly in the U.K. In the long term such research is not expensive, yet its effects on all concerned can be profound. This also applies to any school. The introduction of certain colours can result in a better staff/student relationship. Professor Harry Wohlfarth is considered to be one of the world's leading colour researchers, but his work needs a lot more recognition and his methods need to be put into more practice to help the many they could benefit today.

Colour and Dyslexia

Dyslexia is now known to affect one in ten people of every class, race and cultural background. A psychologist who is Britain's leading expert on the condition defines it as a congenital organising disability which impairs hand skills, short term memory and perception, and thus inhibits reading, writing and spelling. Its effects can range from slight reading or spelling difficulties to complete illiteracy. Helen Irlen, a psychologist from California, discovered during research on adult students with reading difficulties that nearly half of them could be helped using coloured filters. Dr Arnold Wilkins of the Medical Research Council's Applied Psychology Unit at Cambridge has carried out experiments which showed that in some cases Helen Irlen's methods using coloured tinted lenses produced measurable improvements in visual reading and a reduction in distortions. The results are helping to move colour into the main stream of optical practice *(see Complementary Notes 3 and 4).*

Universities and Colleges

When the right colours are introduced into these establishments it can help the students a thousandfold.

Colours introduced into the university or college would encourage the specific area of study, be it classics, law, computer studies, or music and the arts etc. Where a lot of study takes place warm yellows mixed with blue (but more yellow than blue) is needed. The colour yellow will induce study, bring clarity and open up new ideas. At a university the paler yellows could be used in the hallways, with royal blue doors, skirting boards etc. and the introduction of a paler blue ceiling to cool and calm the mind. Only whilst the mind is still can we be inspired; all those who meditate are aware of this. For the classrooms, continue the colour scheme, but in the hallways magenta chairs could be introduced to give the atmosphere some depth. Some blue needs to be introduced into the classrooms, which should not be painted with completely yellow walls.

Where the studies taking place are mainly music and the arts use warm orange colours with blue or blue violet. The main hallway should be in a paler orange, apricot or peach with royal blue introduced for the doors, skirting boards and surrounds with, I suggest, a paler blue ceiling. All the chairs should be blue but any other accessories in a warm tone. In the classrooms follow through with this colour scheme and introduce pictures and murals to add other colours and interest.

In the 'Meeting House' at Sussex University (See colour photograph - page 107) colour has been used with great effect. The circular building, which has a moat around it, was designed by Sir Basil Spence, the architect of Coventry Cathedral. Inside the building is a quiet room which is open to anyone to sit and enjoy some peace; during the evenings, however, there is a wide range of activities including meetings of Student Societies that take place. Upstairs is the chapel, used by many different denominations; and it is also used for music and drama.

As you enter the chapel you are immediately surrounded by all the rainbow colours. Coloured glass is set into pre-cast concrete blocks forming a honeycomb pattern. The glass is German 'antique' specially made for the building. The colours range from blues and greens towards the east through yellows and oranges at the meridian to reds and purples towards the setting sun. The mood of the room changes as the sun shines through different bands of colour; the colours shine brightly inside and at night with the lights on they shine from the outside like a coloured beacon.

Light is also directed onto the altar area through the rooflight which is designed in the form of an eye. Below the organ hangs a tapestry by John Piper and in the middle is depicted the sun following the theme of the room. The interior can take on many moods depending on the time of day and the season of the year, as the light changes in quality and depth.

What surprised me was the quiet room, which was virtually colourless. Here, soothing and relaxing colours could have been introduced - we need to take into consideration the feeling of a whole building, and not just its parts, to create a balanced and integrated environment.

Stained glass is one of the most effective ways of introducing the colours and should be used more widely in the environment; in the long run it is cost effective for our health. Everyone responds when they see colour displayed in this way, and it can have a profound and meaningful effect on us all. We look in wonder when we see a rainbow; the realisation that we are immersed in these colours all the time should make us think more deeply about life.

When colour is used in some of the ways I have suggested here our energies are balanced on many levels. At the moment the education system is very "left brained" offering studying, learning and absorbing knowledge, some of which we shall never use again. The right brain develops our creativity, music, the arts and our intuition. So many people today are either left or right brained; but we need to use both, and become a balanced, whole person. When we incorporate all the colours and their qualities the energy fields around us open up to other areas of development. The following lists some of the positive aspects of the colours - you may find this useful for quick reference.

Colour	Positive Aspect
Red	Courage and strength
Orange	Creative expression, communication
Pale Orange	See Peach and Apricot
Yellow	Clarity, ideas
Pale Yellow	Philosophical ideas
Green	Balance and harmony
Pale Green	Eternal youth
Blue	Opens up our finer feelings and thoughts
Pale Blue	Relaxing - peace, releases stress
Violet	Induces greater intuitive creativity
Pale violet	Spiritual awareness

Other colours I have mentioned:

Royal Blue	Increases our integrity and inner perceptions
Apricot	Creative ideas
Peach	Artistic awareness
Pink	Warming - caring
Rose Pink	Warming, relaxing
Magenta	Lifts the mind from the mundane to a higher purpose

The paler colours do not have the same intensity, but do act as a balance to another colour or its parent colour. Paler colours when used on their own give off very little energy, although they look pleasing. When a warm colour from the colour ray is used, most effective results are obtained.

Red has to be used with caution in the environment today; there is so much violence in our society. This colour excites and activates us emotionally and some people are easily susceptible. At one time we could have used this colour to great effect; we shall do so again.

However, pinks create feelings within us of warmth and caring for other people and for the society we live in. There are wonderful, positive attributes of red, and it is the colour linked to the life force energy. Every pioneer has some red within the aura; it can bring out the adventurous spirit within us, and when used constructively only good can come of it. But when the red ray is suppressed over a period of time and an individual sees the red colour, they may become aggressive, which can eventually lead to violence.

In time to come, we are also going to have to rethink the products we use for furniture and accessories. Rooms should be furnished with natural woods, not vinyl or plastic. Both have their uses and are functional, but we need to surround ourselves with more natural products which give off an energy harmonious with our aura, the electomagnetic energy field that surrounds us.

Complementary Notes

1. The Institute of HeartMath,
    Professor Harry Wohlfarth, M.F.A., D.A., F.I.A.L., F.I.A.C.S. is at the
    University of Alberta, Edmonton, Canada T6G 2T4

2. Research has shown that warm, bright yellow and orange colours will
    improve the intelligence of school age children. Care must be taken as to
    the amount of yellow used.

3. Autistic children need softer tones. Their nervous system is highly-
    charged so care must be taken in deciding which colour tones to use.
    They need some peach, turquoise or greens.

4. British Dyslexia Association, 98 London Road, Reading, Berkshire
    England RG1 5AU.

5. For more information on the work of Helen Irlen read "Reading by the
    Colours" by Helen Irlen, published by Avery and distributed in Britain
    by Worldwide Media Service c/o Biblios Ltd, Star Road, Partridge Green,
    Horsham, West Sussex RH13 8LD.

Chapter 5 Colour and Health Care

Hospitals

The reception area to a hospital needs to be welcoming. When too many blue colours are used it can activate an individual's worst fears, which may seem strange, as blue is known as a healing colour for it can calm and even sedate.

But all colours have dualistic attributes, and the other aspect of blue can bring up hidden fears. When a pale tint from the red or orange rays is used as a main colour an atmosphere of warmth is created, which helps to relax those who are admitted into the hospital as well as relatives and friends who may visit the patient.

Today, as we know, nursing staff and doctors are overworked; in fact, in many cases they are working on overdrive. The suggested warm colours would help them to relax into the work and they would then feel better. Blue can be used to complement the warm tints - preferably a deep blue which gives strength and purpose as well as radiating a healing energy. The window frames, doors, skirting boards and chairs can be painted blue and any artwork can incorporate these two colours and others as well.

Turquoise (which has blue and green within it) when used as a main colour helps to calm the nervous system and then one automatically unwinds. As a main colour it needs to be used much more today, particularly in any health care centre. This colour has a calming effect on the emotions. Complement turquoise with warm tints in the same way I have mentioned above, always maintaining the balance of warm and cool colours together. Do not use yellow as a main colour for the entrance hall or in a waiting area, as this colour affects the mind. People waiting there too long could become stressed and agitated, dwelling more and more upon their symptoms; this could even cause friction between the patients and staff. However, under different circumstances yellow is most effective (see Colour and Education).

Red can be used on the outside of a hospital but inside it must be used with caution. A new hospital I visited in the North of England some time ago had red hand rails and skirting boards in the corridors. Although the area was spacious, patients and visitors entering the hospital would be immediately affected emotionally. Even though red was just introduced in the way described and the walls were a neutral colour, it was enough to activate response. I saw patients holding onto the red hand rails moving from one area to another. Red will energise; but for patients with a heart problem it will over stimulate. Blue hand rails and skirting boards with one of the peach colourings as the main colour for the walls would create a warm, friendly and - most important of all - inviting environment.

Avoid creating a clinical feeling by using too many cool colours. Although calming and soothing in one way, people need to feel emotionally cared for - and that applies to the staff as well. I suggest brown, darker colours (ie. shades in which quite a lot of black has been added to the colour) and any dark greys should not be used where people are unwell. They can have an adverse effect upon us, and one can start to absorb the negative attributes of the colours (see "Know Yourself Through Colour " by the author). White, cream and pale greys, when used with a vibrant colour, can be most effective; they enhance the colouring. Hospitals today are changing and they are looking for ways to brighten up their surroundings. Money permitting, art projects have started with schemes to purchase or commission paintings and drawings to hang on the walls, in order to provide decoration and to improve the general appearance of the building. Using colour, design and art together is most effective. When a new building is about to be built, from the beginning money should be set aside for development or refurbishment. Until a sum is included within budgets in this way such work will continue to be done in a haphazard fashion. For anyone giving a face-lift to an old hospital, I suggest you find a person to advise you who is knowledgeable about the psychology of colour - the difference to the atmosphere and the wellbeing of those who are patients or staff within will be considerable.

A new DHSS hospital built in the Isle of Wight - St Mary's - was designed with a lot of thought. Those involved took into account the whole environment, including the courtyard and gardens which were individually laid out to bring year round visual interest, bringing daylight and colour into the building. Most of the wards were designed with views on to the lake, which was formerly a silted up pond, but is now an attractive wildlife area. St Mary's is known as 'the pathfinder hospital for the nineties' because it has so many innovative ideas introduced into its design, including, and I quote, that 'it is the world's first low energy hospital, designed to cut fuel costs.' In its first year the energy saved was about 40%.

I went with a friend to see the hospital and we were shown around by Guy Eades, the Director of the Healing Arts. A team which included architects, designers and colour specialists integrated the arts, architecture and the environment. The hospital shows what can be done when several people get together with their individual skills and sensitivity to new ideas and are allowed to carry them out. Apparently there was quite a lot of controversy about the colours to be used, but I thought overall the schemes were good, except in one or two areas which I mentioned to Guy. They realised that visual beauty and stimulating surroundings are very therapeutic. The outside of the building does look futuristic, and inside a lot of thought has gone into creating different atmospheres, which made it all the more interesting. Three themes were chosen to demonstrate aspects of the Island, which were in turn reflected in the interior design. Each of the three floors had its own main colour scheme. On the ground floor the theme was 'sea and sand', and they used blue and yellow; on the next floor the theme was 'the landscape' and the colours were mainly green and yellow; for the top floor they used 'buildings' as the theme, reflecting the art work within the building, and the main colours used were pink, orange and red tones used with other colours.

In the reception area on the ground floor a wonderful tapestry adorns a wall going up the stairs, based on a design by Condace Hahouth. It shows the sea life off The Needles, and is a community project and beautifully done. The tapestry has pictures of the sand, the sea, the boats and yachts, ships and the white cliffs etc. Even the floor of the main reception area gave one a feeling of the waves of the sea. My only comment was that too much blue had been used in the decor on the ground floor; it needed a warmer atmosphere. Colour was used to direct you to your destination and to the various departments, and having been lost in many hospitals I thought this was a brilliant idea.

People remember visual impressions far more than directions to read. I was very interested in the colour scheme for the geriatric ward, which mainly used peach colours - warm but not too stimulating, enough to keep the patients awake. The place looked bright and cheerful and so did the patients, compared to other places I have visited.

The dining area was too grey/blue and it appeared cold. The floor and chairs were all in the same colour except the window frames, which were painted in red; too stimulating for unwell patients, and orange would have been better. Blue is not a good colour for dining areas in these sort of environments. It makes our stomachs contract, whereas we need to feel warm inside to digest and enjoy the food. As this dining area, like many others, is the centre of the place it could have incorporated many of the different colours used throughout the building. In another area where we had coffee the pale grey chairs and tables were offset with a vibrant yellow; not too much but enough to be aware of it, and the area would feel sunny even on a dismal day.

The children's section was a delight; here they had used many colours -including a lot of art work - to create a pleasant atmosphere in which a child would feel safe and secure.

The visual art works throughout the building are wonderful. It is reputed that there are 1,000 such works, and much of the credit for this goes to Guy Eades. St Mary's also involves the community in its activities.   Recitals, dance and theatre productions as well as story-telling sessions are held in the day rooms attached to the wards with the co-operation of the doctors and nursing staff. At St Mary's the effects are most noticeable. Staff as well as patients are well aware of the difference art (as in colour, design, murals and pictures etc) has made to the whole project and are proud of it. The team that was responsible for pioneering this project has created much more than a hospital environment, as people in the area have become more involved with its activities. The fear of hospitals, which many people can have, seems to have gone so instead of it being an isolated community it has become very much a part of the main community and a friendly place to visit.

We need more hospitals of this kind - the most important ingredient for success is the commitment of individual managers to introduce some art into hospitals. Once that initial hurdle is overcome the enthusiasm of patients and staff will propel the ideas forward, making it easier to allocate the funds. This was stressed by Mike Ruane, former general manager of the Central Manchester District Health Authority. Many staff, some of them initially dubious about the value of the arts in health care, have testified to the positive changes that have occurred in their patients' behaviour as a result of improvement to their environment and their involvement in arts activities. It must, however, be taken into account with any group of patients that improvements to their visual surroundings need to be carefully considered to match emotional needs. There are signs that such approaches are beginning. For example, at St Luke's Hospital in Bradford the arts programme - as part of the Caring Arts Project - includes colour co-ordinated duvet covers, bed screens and window curtains in the paediatric department and child development centre. At the new Wansbeck General Hospital in Ashington, Northumberland, the theme chosen for all the arts projects was based on the four elements and these are integrated into all aspects of the hospital's design, from curtain fabric to special effects.

Kirklands Hospital for the mentally handicapped in the town of Bothwell, near Glasgow, was designed on a model village. In the centre of the village - which acts as an informal meeting place - there stands a large whale and fish sculpture, created out of cement, stainless steel and bronze. The artist was Fiona Dean. Another artist created an ingenious red, yellow and blue sensory chair. On this piece of sculpture residents can sit and, if they wish, make musical sounds on the tubular components of the sculpture, or identify the colours used by the artist. The chair is also accessible to those who are confined to wheelchairs. What inspiration! For further information on what is being done in hospitals today refer to 'Helping to Heal - the Arts in Healthcare.' (see Complementary Note 2).

Psychiatric Unit

Research has shown that persons troubled with nervous and mental disorders are greatly affected by colour, and respond to it very well. Mental patients are suffering from total collapse of reality as they perceive it. Yellow should not be used in these situations, for the colour stimulates the mind.

Mentally disturbed patients respond to blue and orange; these colours complement and balance each other. People often find the orange hue a difficult colour, but when introduced as a paler orange they like it, as in tints such as peach and apricot. Pink colouring can be used but it is not as effective as the pale orange colour. The main colour in these wards or rooms can be blue, with pale blue ceilings and paler orange colours for curtains, bed screens etc. Paler orange can also be used for the doors and window frames, for it is important to have warmth; too much blue and the patients will withdraw further into their own world. The colours can be reversed by using pale orange for the walls, window frames and doors and blue for the curtains, screens and a pale blue ceiling.

A turquoise colour may be introduced instead of blue for patients who are a lot better but still need some care - but it should have more blue than green within it. In the day room, a stronger orange colour can be used. This will help to bring up and release the past. Counsellors will find patients more willing to talk through their problems. The use of coloured light can be effective in day rooms, but do seek the advice of a *qualified colour therapist.*

Light is known to have a more powerful effect on a person than just using colour in decor as described. Patients will also vary in the way they respond; we are all different (see chapter on Lighting).

Cool colours influence a change in the blood pressure, and when a person likes the colour his whole system becomes relaxed; his outlook and attitude changes. The more emotional patients will react freely to colour in general.

Most people can be grouped by colour preferences; those who prefer cool colours and those who prefer warm colours. Warm colour people are more affected by outside influences and submerge themselves in their social environment. Those who prefer cool colours find it difficult to express themselves freely; emotionally they are cold and reserved and do not even adapt to a change of environment. We need to integrate the warm and cool colours within us. Years ago, when my own marriage broke up and everything else seemed to disintegrate within me, I was always drawn to blue and felt myself becoming aloof. I didn't want to meet people or go out. I knew inwardly I needed some of the orange colour, and decided to introduce it into my kitchen as kitchen bowls and utensils. Many times I thought I would change the colour - this is normal, for the colour you need you often reject - but I didn't. It was only later that I realised how I had changed. After a few months I was going out and meeting people. This was a valuable experience for me, which I have shared with many people.

More and more people realise that mental, emotional and physical health are closely related; colour can activate, vivify, inspire, calm and sedate us. Because of the increased pressure today more and more people are going to need psychiatric help. So often words become meaningless, but colour can penetrate the deepest recesses of our minds so that we can re-evaluate our lives, and then we can decide in which direction we want to go.

Blackthorne Medical Centre, Maidstone, Kent

This is a medical centre which is being run along very different lines and gives one insight into what can be done when the necessary thought, energy inspiration and dedication is put into such work. Owned by the Blackthorn Trust which was founded in 1985, it is concerned with medical care, rehabilitation and the social welfare of patients suffering any serious or long term illness; the conditions treated there range from cancer, Aids and multiple sclerosis to chronic states of anxiety and depression. The Trust works closely with an NHS practice of four doctors. Patients either refer themselves, or come on the suggestion of their own GP or hospital specialist, usually when conventional treatments are not working.

The Centre is built on a redundant hospital site which belonged to the Health Authority, and was opened three years ago. The old psychiatric wing was derelict but had a mature garden and greenhouses, which are now being used by the Centre and which provide work for people recovering from long-term psychological illnesses.

The Centre's architect, Wolodymir Radysh, works for the Camphill Trust *(See Complementary Note 4)* and is one of the few practitioners in the U.K. with a lot of experience with people having special needs. He looks at form, colour and space and what these mean to people. The Camphill approach is based upon Rudolf Steiner's work. The design of this building - particularly inside, which has a curved staircase to the upper floor from reception not unlike an hotel - gives a feeling of welcome and this is reciprocated by those who work there. The waiting area is mainly blue; and although some pink tones have been introduced, I would like to have seen more warmth. Two tapestries given by a patient hang on both sides of the walls. These are beautifully done and give the area depth and interest. The overall colour scheme is mainly pink and blue but I was surprised to see red curtains in the doctors' surgeries. Peach/mushroom doors and one corridor with turquoise walls provided colours which looked lovely together. A special technique has been used to apply the colours to give an unusual effect. The light fittings were designed by the architect, Wolodymir Radysh ; these were most unusual, and yet blended with the overall design of the place.

After they recover, many patients go back to help in any way they can and that the Centre is now a community of people working, sharing, supporting and caring for others is obvious. Outside, the garden has a pond and large greenhouses - these are looked after by many willing hands. One of the outside buildings has now been turned into a bakery serving fresh, home baked bread and cakes every day, and there is also a cafe which serves lunches and includes organically-grown vegetables from the garden. The food is delicious and all this activity serves to bring back a person's self confidence.

The practice has four doctors and apart from the usual, conventional medicine they prescribe other natural remedies, referring patients to complementary therapies when indicated, including music and art therapy. The Centre includes a practice nurse, two district nurses, a midwife, nursing assistant and two health visitors. There are well person clinics, sessions for family planning and dieting. It is not surprising that the Centre was judged by the Royal College of GP's to be the outstanding provider of mental health care by a primary care team.

This Centre has also carried its approach of holistic health into all the materials used; no synthetic materials, only natural plasters, woollen carpets, and organic paints were used. Synthetics give off static electricity and are the underlying cause of a lot of ill health today; until we start to think holistically, we shall only be dealing with the effect and not the cause. The government has formed a think tank to look into health care as offered by the Blackthorne Medical Centre and four other Centres; let us hope this achieves a positive result *(see Complementary Note 3).*

Page 59/60 shows our reactions to some of the colours, which can vary from person to person.

An overview of our reactions to some of the colours

Colour	General Appearance	Emotional Reactions	Mental Reactions
RED	Bright	Warm Over stimulating	Activating Disturbing
ORANGE	Warm	Energising Exciting	Creative Communication
YELLOW	Sunlight	Expansive No boundaries	Alert Radiates
GREEN	Nature	Calming Stillness	Openness Growth
TURQUOISE	Restful	Relaxing Soothing	Spacious Releasing
BLUE	Cooling	Peaceful Aloneness	Thoughtful Introspective
VIOLET	Depth	Devotion Reverence	Meditative Magical
MAGENTA	Majestic	Inspiring Uplifting	In control Spiritual Awareness
WHITE	Light	Brightness Cool	Cleanliness Purity
BLACK	Dark	Depressive Fearful	Uknown Void
GREY	Dull	Unhappy No self worth	Negative Indecisive

Colours and some of their therapeutic effects

RED

Energises, activates the emotions, increases the blood pressure and affects the muscular system.

PINK

Tranquilising, relaxes the muscles, reduces tension, calms the emotions.

ORANGE

Stimulates the mind, can release blocked emotions, encourages a person to be outgoing.

PEACH

Activates creative impulses, induces better relationships.

YELLOW

Stimulates the nervous system, changes pessimism to optimism; too much of this colour overcharges the system.

GREEN

Touches deep-seated emotions, can start to release past traumas - induces peace and harmony.

BLUE

Calms and heals the mind, reduces blood pressure and gives one a greater awareness.

ROYAL BLUE

Healing for the mind, giving a greater depth to the sense of integrity.

TURQUOISE

Relaxing, cooling, soothing for the nervous system. Helps a person to cope with life. Releases inadequacies.

VIOLET

Can help with mental and emotional depression, purges the past to make way for a new beginning.

MAGENTA

Uplifts a person emotionally, mentally and spiritually.

Hospices, Clinics and Health Centres

An atmosphere can be changed by introducing different kinds of art works. An enterprising person could set up a scheme in which pictures etc. which are appropriate for health care environments could be hired out for a certain length of time. (This could, in fact, already be happening). The pictures could cover themes and be hired out either individually or in sets. They could convey a story; the children's area could have nursery rhymes or some of the Walt Disney characters. For adults, pictures could be of beautiful landscapes, gardens and so on. It would be important to introduce a feeling of continuity. Even pictures of butterflies and birds could give a feeling of open spaces and freedom. We associate with what we see; and such sights would become talking points between staff and patients. Sometimes local artists could be involved to create a community venture. See 'Helping to Heal - the Arts in Health Care' which has already been mentioned with regard to funding for some of these ideas.

Such a place should always appear warm and friendly; do not be afraid of using the pure hue of the colour with its paler tints. The deeper the colour the more effect it has on people. Royal blue windows, frames, doors and skirting boards give a healing energy to the place and whatever colour you choose will be enhanced. It is necessary to have as much daylight as possible.

Stained glass could be used in a position where the sun shines through during part of the day. The colour will infuse the whole room and the people in it. Using royal blues, golden yellows, vibrant oranges, greens, reds and violet colours artists could create their own designs to bring these colours into an environment which would help patients to feel better.

When choosing colours, think of nature; green floors, blue skies and in between, all the colours which include thousands of different shades. It is said that in Ancient Egypt, nature was copied in this way. Today we have mixed the colours so much that we use them in any and every way, from blue carpets to green ceilings. Perhaps we should take a look at this and review our way of thinking. As human beings, we are always trying to change everything. I don't feel it has got us very far - when we look around us we see a world in chaos. Perhaps we should copy nature and start to reintroduce a state of harmony into our own environment.

Day Centres for intensive probation programmes designed to reduce offending behaviour

The colours I suggest should be used for such centres are ORANGE, BLUE and GREEN used with white or off white. Do not use both blue and green in the same room.

ORANGE — Use mainly warm peach colours; this colour vibration will get to the basic cause of the behaviour which needs correcting. It also increases creativity, and with it different kinds of music and art therapy can be introduced.

BLUE — Use royal blue for the skirtings, doors etc. and in some rooms use a pale blue ceiling. There are many tones of blue and they create a calming, relaxing and sedating atmosphere.

GREEN — Use green as the main colour for the recreation room. It will create a feeling of peace and balance and its use with the peach colour will give the room some warmth.

For the discussion room introduce warm peach colours with some blue tones and use pink and blue lights with the ratio of 2 blue to 1 pink (see Lighting). These can be used separately or together; the pink light contributes a non-agressive and non-intrusive influence and the blue light is tranquillising.

Drugs and Alcoholic Centres

The colours I suggest should be used for these Centres are SALMON PINK and LAVENDER BLUE used with white or off white.

SALMON PINK — The vibration of universal love and self love.

LAVENDER BLUE — Awakens the person to a deeper meaning and gives them a purpose to life.

AVOID USING GREEN IN THE DECOR for these Centres; this will awaken deep seated emotions and so be traumatic for recovering addicts. Their healing needs to be gradual, otherwise they will revert to the old patterns.

With addictions of this kind, the sufferer is trying to cut off the emotions and the mind. Addiction is a form of running away; the addict finds him or herself unable to cope with reality. Colour within these environments will help the recovering addict to find his or her true self.

For the recreation rooms in these Centres use pink and blue spotlights, in the ratio of two pink to one blue.

Do remember you can use the different tones of all the colours in each instance.

Maternity Units

Always use a pale colour of the red and blue rays to create an atmosphere that is relaxing and warm. These colours are also more in tune with the auric colours surrounding mother and baby. I am aware that many hospitals today have used some lovely colours in these units. There are many combinations; for instance, when you use pink, then surround the door with a darker pink. It looks most effective and a pale blue ceiling will bring a calming effect on both the mother and child. Babies could be put into pink sheets and blankets - the colour that is linked to love. Many mothers today also need extra loving care so pink curtains would let them relax and let go for a while. Today many fathers witness the birth of their baby, so the image of the father walking up and down in a waiting room is not so applicable as it used to be. The colours introduced into these areas are important; a lovely turquoise with pale yellow and pale rose pink will calm the nervous system, the mind and the emotions respectively. This area would then also create a welcoming environment for relatives and friends.

Intensive Care Unit

The interests of those who take care of the patients must be considered as well as the patients themselves in intensive care. The nursing staff are on duty around the clock. To use pink colourings with blue to complement is good - green would be draining for long periods. Many different colours of blue could be used and to have a pale blue ceiling would be calming for all concerned.

Coloured lights could be used in this environment as these can be adjusted and turned on and off as required. A coloured light would infuse the whole room. or coloured lights can be directed where necessary towards a patient.

IMPORTANT - *before going ahead, consult a qualified colour therapist.*

After Intensive Care

When a patient is moved to another room after being in the intensive care unit, warm peach colours with turquoise would help them to feel both safe and relaxed. Later, if a patient has to stay longer in hospital to convalesce, then they should be in a ward or room decorated with some pink, apple green or pale yellow. This would enable them to reorientate themselves (yellow) for when they leave the hospital, relax (green) and feel warmth (pink) and that life holds a lot of good things to come.

Operating Theatre

Usually this room is painted green to offset the red colour of blood, and the surgeon also wears a green gown. Green as an energy will have a calming effect on all those present, but when they have to be in the theatre for a long time green will tend to drain a person's energy. A turquoise colour, which has both green and blue within it, would be cooling and relaxing, and this colour is not draining. The surgeon's gowns could also be in this colour. Turquoise releases tension and stress and is a very healing colour. The adjoining room to the theatre could also be painted in this colour, with peach or peachy pink. The effect on the patient would be instant; even though half sedated, they would still receive the energy from such surroundings.

Doctors' and Dentists' Practices

Most practices play safe and have very neutral colours in their waiting rooms and in the surgery. I feel that often, unless they are part of a unit, they do not bother about colours - as long as people have somewhere to sit down and a few magazines to look at they are fine. But the difference when the waiting room is given some consideration would have far reaching consequences. Not only could the patients be more relaxed on seeing the doctor or dentist but the practitioner themselves would feel different in a calming and relaxing environment. *Do not use yellow in a dentist's surgery as research from America has shown it makes a patient more conscious of pain.*

The Surgery

It is most important that the actual surgery imparts the feeling of a person who is relaxed and cares about his patients. The following are a few ideas for schemes which would be most effective.

Turquoise and peach and white or off white

Blue and rose pink and off white

Green and peach or pink and white or off white

Choose the cooler colour for the main colour (green can be either) and this can be used for the doors, windows, skirting boards etc. with walls either white or a paler colour of the main colour. Use the warm colour for curtains and any accessories. In the doctor's surgery the colour for the chairs should be blue, and in the dentist's surgery the chair could be in royal blue. This would really calm the patient down and help them to immediately relax. However the rest of the room needs to be in a warm colour, although the doors and windows can also be in a royal or paler blue. One has to remember that there are so many colour variations, and so many colourings within a colour; so you are not restricted.

It is the waiting room area which is so important. Introduce some pictures that are interesting to look at; they can be colourful, but make sure they are not arousing to look at. Pink, as a colour, will calm a person's worst fears, but if you do not want pink then introduce a peachy pink colour. Where there is a separate room for receptionist, make sure you follow through with the colour scheme to create a balanced and harmonious environment.

Therapy Rooms

Complementary medicine today is widespread and many disciplines are being practised. The decor in a therapy room will affect not only the patient/client but also the therapist.

In choosing colours for your room, do take into consideration the type of treatments or therapy you practise.

Aromatherapy and Massage Therapy

For these treatments a massage table is required, so you would be well advised to choose a pale blue ceiling since this colour is very relaxing for both you and your patient/client. As the person receiving the treatment looks upward towards the ceiling it will have a very calming effect. The windows, skirtings and doors can also be painted pale blue, but the rest of the room needs a warm colouring.

Acupuncture

I would advise similar colourings as described above. The fear of the treatment being so often worse than the actual treatment, a warm pink colour for the walls also helps to relax the patient and reduce that fear.

Osteopathy and Chiropractic

Some blue in the room will help to reduce any pain; blue, in colour therapy, is known as the greatest healing colour, for its effect can be instant. The introduction of royal blue windows, skirtings and doors will start to release within the person the initial cause of the problem; how it started. The displacement of joints, for example, is only the effect. The blue colour will help the patient to let go and release inner tension and stress. The therapist will then have a deeper insight into the initial cause, as the patient will talk about his or her problems. The walls can be decorated in a warm pink/peach and the ceiling in a pale blue or white.

Homeopathy and Herbalism

Introduce a green colour into the decor. Apple green affects the heart and emotions, and a person becomes more receptive to the treatment. Sometimes patients are encouraged by a friend to go and have a treatment, knowing little about the therapy, and this can sometimes block the good the therapies can do for them. The unconscious remembers everything and associates it accordingly.

GREEN IS ASSOCIATED WITH HARMONY, HOPE AND FREEDOM.

Decide on the main colour and complement it with another colour, using its paler tint. Where possible I recommend a pale blue ceiling but this would depend on the whole colour scheme.* The windows, skirtings and doors can be either in white or a paler or darker shade of the main colour chosen. There are many choices to be made, so have some fun! Do also remember that the amount of light entering the room will affect its colours; a dark room needs lighter and brighter colourings.*

In the colour co-ordinated rooms I have suggested, use white paint for the tables and also white for drawers or filing cabinets. They will be most effective. Where natural woods are used in your room then use off white paint (if that is your choice) - do try to avoid darker woods, which make a room look sombre.

We see the colour on the walls as static but it emits an energy, and is affecting us all the time, whether we are aware of this or not. Colours need to blend and meld together, and it is so important to use colours which complement each other (see the Colour Wheel, page 101).

The following are colour co-ordinated suggestions for your Therapy Rooms. Choose three colours (I include white as a colour). You will still have many variations to choose from as each colour has so many shades and tints.

You will also notice that the colour of the screens and chairs blend into the carpet colour in rooms one and two, but the colours for these contrast each other in rooms three and four. This is because where a pale blue ceiling is used it changes the energy.

*   Do not use blue and green together

Room One

Colours: peach, turquoise and white

	PEACH	TURQUOISE	WHITE or OFF WHITE
Ceiling			X
Walls	X		
Carpets		X	
Curtains		X	
Lampshades	X		
Tables			X or natural wood
Towels (if required)	X		
Screens		X	
Chairs		X	
Accessories	X*		

* If no screen is used, use turquoise for accessories.

Windows, skirtings and doors pale turquoise or white.

NB. You can use turquoise for the walls instead of peach, in which case just change the colours accordingly.

Room Two

Colours: pink, green and white

	PINK	GREEN	WHITE or OFF WHITE
Ceiling			X
Walls	Warm pink		
Carpets		Apple green	
Curtains		X	
Lampshades	X		
Tables			X or natural wood
Towels (if required)	X		
Screens		Apple green	
Chairs		X	
Accessories	X		

Windows, skirtings and doors white or pale green.

Room Three

Colours: yellow, blue/violet and white

	YELLOW	BLUE/VIOLET	WHITE or OFF WHITE
Ceiling		Pale blue	
Walls			X
Carpets	Golden yellow		
Curtains	Yellow edged blue/violet		
Lampshades		Pink*	
Tables			X or natural wood
Towels (if required)**			
Screens		Blue/violet	
Chairs		Blue/violet	
Accessories	X		

* Pink lampshades are warmer than yellow, and are therefore better

** Pink towels

Windows, skirtings and doors yellow to blend in with the carpet.

Room Four

Colours: blue, pink and white

	BLUE	PINK	WHITE or OFF WHITE
Ceiling	Pale blue		
Walls		X	
Carpets		Rose pink	
Curtains	Blue/pink		
Lampshades		X	
Tables			X or natural wood
Towels (if required)		Rose pink	
Screens	Pale blue		
Chairs	X		
Accessories	X*		

Windows, skirtings and doors pale blue.

*When you use a colour massage table make sure the colour blends in with the rest of the scheme.

Complementary Notes

1. *Doctors and dentists who use a white coat in your practice; use a warm blue coat instead. It will help you to relax and will have a calming effect on your patients.*

2. ** I recommend 'Helping to Heal, the Arts in Healthcare' by Peter Senior and Johnathan Croall, published by the Gulbenkian Foundation, London 1993. It supplies information on what is going on in hospitals today. This illustrated book covers so many aspects of health care, even information on how to go about funding a project and who to approach. I found the contents uplifting - so much is already being done but so much more could be accomplished by those who have the vision to carry it out.*

3. *Blackthorne Medical Centre, St Andrew's Road, Maidstone, Kent, England ME16 9AN.*

4. *Wolodymir Radysh, Camphill Architects, Newton Dee, Bieldside, Aberdeen, Scotland AB1 9DX.*

Chapter6: Colour - Its Application Within the Commercial Environment

We have created a wide range of commercial environments in which to work and each of these needs its own particular atmosphere. In this chapter I take a look at a selection of commercial situations and the effects of colour on each.

Factories

In industry today there is a very high rate of absenteeism due to ill health - and most of this is caused by stress. Factories in which there is a lot of noise affect the nervous system. Blue has a calming effect on the whole system, so painting machines a royal blue will help the operator. The walls should be a warm colour such as peach or apricot, but never use red near machines. The electromagnetic field will become over-energised with the red ray and this can have an adverse effect upon some people - it can result in mistakes being made.

Factories need to be light and airy as well as colourful, without being too bright - a place that is too bright will divert the concentration from the task in hand. Depending upon how much light there is in the building, a pale blue ceiling has a calming effect on the mind; I suggest you introduce a green colour for the floor because its vibration is more restful for the feet. These in turn affect the rest of the body so green is a better colour to use for the floor than grey, brown or terracotta in this situation. Where a place has dark floors and equipment use pale colours for the walls. Other colour choices would depend upon the activity taking place within that environment. For instance, a textile company in which a lot of colour is used in the fabric manufacturing process should introduce turquoise. This cooling colour will offset the vibrations from the mixture of so many hues which can over-energise a person. Peach would go well with turquoise here - it would encourage those who work in the environment to appreciate and enjoy their work, as peach is such a creative colour.

In Toronto, Canada, fashion designer and women's clothes manufacturer Linda Lundstrom had many machines in a factory which kept breaking down. Each repair was proving very costly. One day she awoke from a dream telling her to cover the machines with turquoise silk. When she suggested this to her directors they thought she was crazy - never mind the idea, it was the total cost they considered far too expensive! Well, she insisted that in the long term it would pay dividends, and one by one the small and large machines were covered in turquoise silk. She told me that since that day the machines have run smoothly except for the occasional need for routine maintenance. She invited me to see her factory and I met her directors. They agreed it seemed to have worked! Incidentally Linda's clothes are lovely and are sold in Canada, the States and parts of Europe. They are not only imaginative but very colourful.

When machines are used by many people the mix of different energies affects the machines. For example, photocopying machines used in the market place by the public seem to need a lot of attention, but it has been proved in some establishments in which only one or two people use the machines that they need less maintenance. Cars tell a similar story; some people find their car needs only routine servicing whereas other vehicles need regular attention from the moment of purchase. This leads me to wonder whose energy was near the car whilst it was being assembled - and we need also to take into account the person who is now driving the car. All energy affects other energy; like the turquoise silk (silk is a good conductor of any energy vibration) which certainly affected the machines at Linda Lundstrom's factory, amazing though this might seem the application of colour worked.

Number one priority when planning a factory should be to create an harmonious environment. When the workforce is happy, production improves. Today so many people are working longer hours; their stress builds up quickly. To have a recreation room for workers, a place they could visit at regular intervals, would relieve some of this stress. You could introduce calming colours of green and turquoise with a warm colour and have a miniature water fountain in the middle of the room (water relaxes the emotions immediately). Even a large fish tank has been known to create an atmosphere of calm. The movement of fish affects our psyche and we automatically relax - so it starts to relieve the inner tension. As time goes on we shall have to look at some of these ways to avoid an energy build up of tension which turns into stress - otherwise everything will eventually break down.

Faber Birren *(see complementary note 1)* was a well known colour consultant in America. He advised education authorities, the armed forces, government offices, architects, industry and commerce with amazing results. According to Birren end walls coloured in medium tones are most effective in factories.

When workers are engaged in difficult tasks to be able to look up and see a pleasing colour can be most relaxing, and it improves efficiency. Colour needs to blend rather than stand out. Birren suggested the use of cool colour such as blue or green where the working conditions are very warm; likewise warm tones if it is cold. This can also compensate for the lack of natural light. Where distractions need to be avoided he used soft greens and blues, and for very high ceilings he suggested a peach colour for all the walls and a darker tone for the ceiling.

Birren devised a Safety Colour Code *as follows;*

Yellow	For falling hazards, to be painted on obstructions, low beams, dead ends, edges of platforms etc.
Orange	For acute hazards, around the edges of cutting machines and rollers.
Green	To identify first aid equipment, cabinets, medicines.
Red	For fire protection devices - and also on valves and fittings for hose connections.
Blue	For caution - switch control boxes.
White	For corners, to discourage litter.

This code was widely employed and it cut down accidents by 60%. Birren's work for the United States Navy has been described as the largest ever single colour co-ordination job. The Safety Colour Code is internationally accepted in many parts of the world to this day. His work was acknowledged and recommended by the Council of

Industrial Health of the American Medical Association. There was a concensus of his work which was so conclusive it proves that colour has a profound effect on individuals and on the environment as a whole.

Mankind's emotional attitude to colour is well known. When a business is without profit, we say it is 'in the red'; we talk of 'red letter days' and when a person 'sees red' they are angry. We associate green with 'green fingers' and we also associate it with jealousy, which shows as an unpleasant green in the aura. With blue, we talk about a person being 'true blue' or having 'blue blood', feeling blue etc. The colours each have a positive and negative attribute, so it is important to use more of the tints than the shades as the latter demonstrates the negative aspect. Research has shown that colour does influence mood and feeling. We can feel happy or sad, joyful, fearful and so on. Colour can affect our pulse and fluctuations in blood pressure as I have already mentioned. The emotional changes which also create the above are triggered by our association with the colour. Red means excitement, whilst we associate green with nature - it is calming and peaceful. Yellow is the sun, blue is the sky and all these are deeply embedded within us. The affect of colour on the emotions creates a spontaneous reaction - we do not think about it. Therefore when the right colours are introduced into a given environment the results are immediate, even if a person does not like the colour. The very fact that there is a response will release feelings - and they can then respond more to the colours they do like.

The colours used to represent a company indicate the intention of that company, but remember we are looking at many different attributes for each colour. Some petrol stations use red and yellow for their colours; red we associate with movement and excitement, and yellow with the mind and the intellect, which could be saying to us "a wise choice to buy your petrol from here". Today many people are using different shades of blue with yellow for inside and the front of their shops; we associate blue with safety and honesty and yellow with choice, so be cautious and think for yourself - it has been known for a long time that colour can and does manipulate us all when we are off guard.

Precincts and Shopping Malls

The terms 'precinct' and 'shopping mall' mean the same depending on which part of the world you live in. In these environments, avoid using red and too many bright colours as they can activate energy and sometimes be the cause of disagreements leading to violence. A few years ago a large precinct was being built in Watford, Hertfordshire; the walls were painted in peach and I watched everyone's reaction. I could see they thought it was lovely, but apparently this was only the undercoat, and later it was painted cream! Turquoise and peach were used around the lifts to great effect. What a shame these colours were not used for the overall effect - it would have been interesting to see how people responded over a period of time.

In some of these places negative energy can build up. In this kind of area a lot of incidents seem to happen which are always unpleasant. Blue and pink lights inserted into the ceiling would help the situation, but use more pink than blue in a ratio of two to one *(See Lighting)*.

Banks

Banks have now become more colourful and it is interesting to see how many of them are using the blue colourings. The message here is 'I am safe, trust me, all is in capable hands'. We could say this use of colour is like using subliminal messages - so do not be taken in by the colours, only by recommendations. Cashiers in banks would be wise to wear blue when at work; it will sometimes help to deter violence should the bank be robbed, for when a person sees blue they tend to pause and think before acting. What is noticeable is that very few have chosen green for their main colour, which is the colour from a psychological point of view that most associate with money. Care must be taken with the use of yellow, as this colour could create disagreements, especially when it comes to money matters as it is the colour linked to the mind. In the bank manager's office introduce a blue wall behind the manager's seat - people will be more open and honest in all their dealings.

Hotels

Most of the big hotel groups today are colour minded - they know that first impressions are important. The way you introduce colours can be your trademark, and if you are part of a group comprising several hotels you could choose three colours with three complementary colours for the whole hotel. This still gives a wide choice with all the different available tones. Use the colours in all your hotels but in different ways. The main thing to decide is what kind of atmosphere you want to create. Choose your colour schemes wisely; people will then always remember the name of the hotel when they see the colours and this can become a very good way to advertise the hotel.

A country hotel would have a different sort of atmosphere - comfort is much more important than elegance and relaxing, comfy chairs in the entrance hall always make a place seem inviting. Depending on the country hotel's situation, autumnal colours can look wonderful; peach, golden colours mixed with greens. Do keep it simple and where possible use natural materials but with different textures. Too many patterns on floors or upholstery will create a busy environment; today people are looking for peace and relaxation, and to let go and release the pressure in their lives even if only for a short while.

When I was working in Ireland I stayed at the Deer Park Hotel, in Houth near Dublin. The colour scheme of the restaurant's lounge was lovely; they had used turquoise and rose pink as the main colours, the chairs were upholstered in turquoise and the settees were covered in woven fabric of cream, turquoise and pink. The curtains were a natural colour and edged with turquoise; the carpet was rose pink and the walls pale turquoise. The use of colour and interesting fabrics gave the room a distinct atmosphere - everyone admired it and found the room inviting, relaxing and comfortable.

Too many bright colours in a foyer can be distracting and a guest can become overcharged, especially if he/she has to sit down and wait - any energy discrepancies in the place can be picked up. I appreciate the attitude of the staff is most important; however, the colours chosen will influence both the staff and the guests.

Bed and breakfast establishments need to get away from the eternal creams, browns, dark orange and muddy yellow colours that so many still use today. Be more venturesome and introduce rose pinks, apricot and pale greens - the warmth of the proprietor is most important but to walk into a place with lovely colours can lift one's spirits, especially after a long journey.

I would advise you not to use red in bars and restaurants today. If you like these colours use the many tones of the colour, and magenta in some environments will completely change the energy of the place.

Offices

When I visited Canada I had the opportunity to look at several offices. They were well appointed but colourless. The ones I saw were in a high rise building and had wonderful views over the city of Toronto but for people to work day after day in a colourless environment has a definite effect. They can easily become tired, irritiable and stressed. We can flourish in a colourful atmosphere, feel refreshed (depending upon the colours) and our responses can be much quicker as we are receiving a stimulus. When designing and decorating an office avoid making it look too artistic - you will defeat the overall effect.

Some time ago I gave a lecture about colour and the environment and after the interval I invited questions. A lady asked if she could share her experience with colour. At the office where she had worked for many years there had been rose pinks, yellows and greens, and people commented when they visited the offices. Then the management changed - they had the offices painted in cream and white with all new office equipment. It looked more modern but was colourless. In no time the harmony that had been in the office before seemed to change; many said it was the change of management but those who worked in the offices had the feeling that if there was more colour everything would be different again. It took four years before the colours were changed and as soon as rose pinks and apple greens were introduced the difference was immediately noticeable. People were more friendly and the management agreed that the work efficiency in the place had increased - they were sorry they had not changed it before.

I hear many stories like this; once in Zurich I was teaching a colour therapy course and a student approached me about the company she was working for. Apparently they had done very well over the last two years and decided to improve the decor. They approached some specialists who advised them to have off white and grey; she said it looked dismal and the business at the present time was not doing too well. I suggested they introduced some pale orange and green colours into the place and on my next visit to Zurich she said they had decided to take my advice and the difference was amazing; everyone was brighter and the business was now doing well again. All this feedback makes one realise the power of colour to change an atmosphere for the better. Your business is only as good as your staff; make them feel good about themselves and they will respond accordingly.

Management are often happy enough to have a colourful logo on their notepaper, but when it comes to their surroundings they do not follow through. Be the colours you say you are on your stationery and introduce them into your environment. That way you are making a positive statement about the company, what you represent and how you feel about yourselves and the product/service you are selling; it could be a tangible product or a less tangible service such as insurance.

The political parties recognise the power of colour but they all need to introduce the complementary colour as well, to act as a balance. I feel it would help them to be more centred in the policies they wish to introduce and maintain. It is so easy to work with the negative side of the colouring; blue can be self righteous, and red too determined to succeed without enough forethought of the execution of policies. Yellow can be too idealistic. In the same way the colours of the national flag represent the country of origin. For Britain red, white and blue; red the pioneer, determined to play its part in world affairs; blue working towards being true to itself and taking responsibility, and white balancing the two energies, linking to spiritual forces for insight and guidance. The amount of colour introduced for any given flag would affect its energy balance. I introduce these aspects to help you to realise that colour influences everything and is the key to understanding ourselves on the deepest levels; our motive intentions and integrity. We must remember, however, that colour, like everything in life, has two sides; positive and negative, and we either work with one or the other.

Huge offices where many people work in one room can be noisy and distracting. Quite often some of these rooms are partitioned off by dividers. When blue is chosen for such partitions do not choose too dark a colour, for each unit will then be segregated from the others. For energy to be balanced there needs to be some form of unity, even if this is at another level of awareness. A medium to light blue - not a cold blue - allows each person his or her own space. Do have a warm colour for the carpets, a different tone for the walls etc. and the third colour, perhaps off white, can be used for the doors, ceilings, window frames and so on. Do not use green for partitions; it will slow down the work too much and not everyone likes green. Turquoise is a good colour to use, very soothing and relaxing, and a different energy from the blue that makes you go inward. Turquoise cools the mind and affects the emotions. Brown partitions are very sombre and can be very depressive; they do not allow any individual to step out of line and they dampen free expression. Staff can become like zombies - yes, they do the work, but it is soul destroying. Keep brown in its natural environment and use only sparingly in these sort of places. You would be surprised to see the initiative and enhanced work from your workforce given the right opportunities - and the best use of colour.

More and more people today have a job out of the home. When we realise that 1/3 of our lives is spent in these environments it should make us think. When I ask people what colours they have in their offices I can't believe it; brown, cream and grey with no other colours. No wonder people go around looking tired and feeling as if they have no energy! I repeat; colour will energise, revitalise, help us to feel happy and enthusiastic about life and see that each day is a new day which holds many opportunities within it. Colour is like electricity - it is out there and within us but is only activated when we plug in and realise that we can utilise it to enhance our lives.

Airports - Aeroplanes

Having just returned from Germany I noticed a lot of green is being used for the chairs in the lounges. Some of the green colours are vibrant and look good, but green does need to be complemented with a warm colouring such as rose pink or even apricot. The rose pink colour looks wonderful with violet tones, another colour I noticed is being used for seating. Magenta could also be used for chairs - although it has some red in it the violet acts as a balance to the red. Magenta and green go together well and enhance each other's energies. Have a different tone of either of these colours for the carpets, which is preferable to grey, black or brown.

Aeroplanes

So many of the interiors of aeroplanes have too much blue in them. Where possible more of the earth colours need to be introduced; for example, a warm peach for the carpet, pale peach for the walls, say turquoise or blue for the seating and any other areas should be light grey ie. the backs of the seats, overhead lockers etc. Different tones of rose pink can be used instead of peach but do keep off reds; they are far too energising and stir the emotions. Rose pink colourings reduce fear and help to relax the passengers. Red is fine on the outside of the aircraft but a lot of thought needs to go into the colour scheme within. Being in the air, where there is a lot of blue sky, sometimes gives people the feeling of floating. The more one can make them feel secure the more the passengers will travel with that airline. A woman's menstrual cycle can be affected by flying, so more warm colours introduced for the inside of the aircraft will help the airline stewardesses; the warm colours ground the energies within us.

Seagoing Liners

In choosing colours for the interiors of a ship use very little blue; being on the ocean, one needs warm colours to feel grounded. Green is a good complementary colour and acts as a backcloth to the other colours. Violet can be used with discretion and with green can give a distinct atmosphere. Shape, form and colour are also important on board ship. Every form has an energy (colour) and this in itself helps to keep people stabilised. All the five platonic solids (see chapter on Shape, Form and Colour) need to be incorporated, which includes the pentagon shape, a transformer of energy.

Colours For a Dramatic Environment

Where you want to create a distinctive atmosphere - in theatres, hotels, restaurants and large establishments etc. - introduce a rich, golden yellow. As you will see below the colour with which you use it creates a meaningful environment.

The following suggestions to use with gold also give you some idea of the mood it will create. I suggest you use paler tones from any of the colours chosen to go with the golden yellow. The intensity of the mood you wish to create will depend upon the depth of the colour. You can use pale cream or off white for the paintwork, according to the environment.

Gold with Red	Pure love
Gold with Orange	Pure joy
Gold with Turquoise	Pure wonderment
Gold with Royal Blue	Pure radiance
Gold and Magenta	Pure magic
Gold with Violet	Pure inspiration

Complementary Notes

1. Faber Birren, 'Colour Psychology and Colour Therapy' Publisher University Books Inc., 1961.

2   Green, blue or turquoise not only reduce nervous tension but also muscular tension. Too much yellow can sometimes make people hyperactive and then later depressed. It has a twofold action; this can also apply to red when used, for it will boost the energy then later it drops lower than before.

3   A big expanse of colour needs always to be complemented with its complementary colour or a contrast colour in a paler tone.

4. Pale blue ceilings give a feeling of expansiveness and awareness but only use within certain environments. Do not have a pale blue ceiling and pale blue walls unless the working conditions are very warm - even then, complement it with a warm hue.

5. Plants and flowers can change the atmosphere of any area, and give a good impression on first arrival at any hotel or theatre etc. They also help to purify an environment as they give off fresh oxygen and help to remove toxic pollutants from the air.

Chapter 7: How Colour Can Reduce Violence and Influence Behaviour Patterns

Not one day goes by without some crime being committed; a murder, a person being raped and so on. I am aware that those in the media feel they have to report on what is happening but so often this gives ideas to people who already have a tendency to crime, especially younger people. Being a reporter, producer or presenter on television or radio holds a lot of responsibility, as does the writing and producing of newspapers, whose editors only seem to want to print sensational news, usually about some dreadful event.

Some films also play their part in contributing to crime and how to do it and now we have the Internet, explaining to those who belong to its network how to go about becoming a criminal, and even the different ways of having sex! What was and is still an amazing information tool is being abused. Only when more people are prepared to look at these issues and do something about them will violence in our society become a thing of the past.

I realise that people must be free to choose what to read and which programmes to watch on television, but it is the younger generation that should concern most responsible adults. As a mother of three grown up children I know how impressionable they can be at an early age; as mine got older they liked to watch programmes which I thought were unsuitable. Some families I know have banned the television from the home. They now find they communicate with each other far more and have also become more creative. One such family reintroduced television as their son felt he was missing out on the programmes his friends watched; they agreed that some were interesting but after a year his behaviour had changed so much. He became irritable, argumentative and difficult, and so the television is now out of this home for good.

Careful choice of colours in the home would bring about a change of interests. The young would then find more creative pursuits in the home and their immediate environment. In time to come, colour psychology will be part of the curriculum in schools and then youngsters will realise the power of some of the forces which surround us all. I do feel that children should be able to choose their own colours for their rooms, however; even if, as some mothers have related to me, they want their bedrooms painted black! Let them paint the rooms black; if you resist, they will insist more. You will find they soon want the rooms repainted, but meanwhile do keep an eye on them, since black can induce sombre, macabre feelings. For some it is a stage they need to go through; but during this stage do keep visualising them in a room full of light in your mind's eye - you might be surprised at the results.

Violence in the Market Place

A large Leisure Centre which is being built on the outskirts of London has 10-foot high royal blue boards placed around it whilst it is being constructed. So far no grafiti or illicit posters have appeared on the boards; just those the contractors have put up. As I have said before, royal blue does act as a deterrent; I have noticed that in some areas some enlightened people have even painted their railings in royal blue. Colour is being used far more today for shop fronts, theatres, restaurants etc.

Yellow seems to be a favourite colour and used with blue, it looks most effective. But always make sure you use more blue than yellow, as yellow activates people's energy - and not always in the right way.

Underground Stations

Colours in underground stations need to be bright, with white walls. Green could be used more for seating - a similar green that is being used for London Airport's lounges, with rose pink or peach colours incorporated into the colour scheme. The outside of the trains should be painted in royal blue, and in environments of this kind avoid using too many grey colourings. The interiors of trains should therefore be off white (white or off white will always reflect the other colours you introduce). One of my students from a course I was giving in London found herself the witness of an unpleasant brawl in an underground station. We had been talking about placing the Light around ourselves, and also what we would do when seeing a situation becoming out of control. She immediately surrounded herself with light and then, in thought, surrounded the four fighting men in deep blue, which I had suggested in class. She continued to do this and found the four men started to break up and move away from each other. We do not actually have to see the light or the colour when acting in this way; thought can be most powerful. Just to think Light and to ask for the colour to go to them was sufficient. It is obviously unwise to stay around people in a fight; but being already in the underground, my student wished to catch her train and then get home as soon as possible. Do remember; if you are on a train and someone tries to molest you, think of the LIGHT; imagine yourself as a light bulb, radiating out light, and you will find that this will have a positive effect.

Whenever I am driving in my car and get stuck behind a large van or lorry I recall a time when I was in a hurry to get to my destination, and wanted to pass a large vehicle in front of me. As the road was very winding it was not easy to overtake, so I had to wait and to be patient. The back of this lorry was painted green, and as I continued to look at it I noticed that I was becoming more and more relaxed. I stopped worrying about whether or not I would be late. I feel that painting the back of large lorries green or blue would be a good idea and could stop a driver from becoming impatient, and maybe even prevent an accident!

Pink Prison Cells

The idea of introducing pink into a prison cell came from America. A director of the Institute for Biosocial Research in Tacoma, Washington, informed delegates at a conference in California that pink, properly applied, relaxes hostile and aggressive individuals in about fifteen minutes. The Naval Correctional Centre in Seattle found that pink walls subdued violent inmates - but experiments have shown that too much exposure to pink can induce an imbalance to the system (pink has a tranquillising effect on the muscular system and calms the emotions).

The colour is called 'Baker-Miller Pink' (some refer to it as 'bubble gum pink') after a police chief called Baker and a psychologist called Miller. A single cell was painted in this shade of pink which radiates a wavelength of 618 nanometers *(see Complementary Note 1).* The ceiling and walls, door and window were painted in gloss pink mixed to the ICI Dulux Code 0040R20B (The Imperial Chemical Industries U.K.) The floor was painted a neutral grey, the cell had a solid door and the window consisted of opaque glass. Artificial lighting was provided by a standard incandescent light bulb, separated by security glass over the door.

The pink cell idea was first introduced into the U.K. by Superintendent Peter Bennett *(See Complementary Note 2)* who had seen the pink cell on one of his visits to New York. A Commissioner who showed him the cell said they were very impressed, as it had such a profound effect on any prisoner placed within it - although if they could find any other way of calming such prisoners they preferred to do so. Several police stations in the U.K. tried this method. To begin with, only every other person who was detained was placed in the pink cell; other prisoners were placed in a cell painted magnolia. Inmates of both cells were monitored by the staff at ten minute intervals and their behaviour recorded. The overall concensus showed a significant level of improvement in behaviour from the prisoner in the pink cell compared to that of the prisoner in the magnolia cell. Later, they used the pink cell for people who were mainly violent; fighting drunk, who had attacked a police officer or who had damaged a cell. The prisoner was left in the cell for about 30 minutes and then returned to another cell, this time painted magnolia. One prisoner in Huddersfield turned from using obscene language to singing hymns; another man, a violent drunk who was a regular client of the station, surprised everyone by his politeness after a period in the pink cell.

Superintendent Bennett felt the pink cell could help long term inmates, but there was a resistance within the Police Force to the pink decorated cell. Since that time pink light has been used instead of painting a cell pink, and this has been just as successful. I would suggest that blue lights be installed in the cell and used after the pink light, which would produce a different kind of calming effect on the prisoner and reduce any side effects which may occur.

Superintendent Bennett and I met on a television programme some time ago. I was introducing the many ways of using colour and he was explaining the results of using the pink cell. The audience was highly amused when he said his colleagues called him the 'Pink Panther'! Like all forms of research, investigations into the use of colour develop from one stage to the next - the pink cell has even been used in New Delhi, India, and they agree that the pink acts as a sedative, affecting the adrenal glands and sending messages to the hypothalamus to slow down secretions which action in turn slows down the heart muscle. But their report indicated that prolonged exposure to the colour can lead to a condition called malillumination, which results in an imbalance in the endocrine system. As a colour therapist I agree with this, and feel that fifteen minutes is long enough for exposure to the pink light. I suggest using the blue light for five minutes, to balance the treatment. Coloured lights are far cheaper than decorating a cell and yet can be most effective; let us hope that this research will continue, because use of lights in this way does far more than have a calming effect - it affects us at the deepest of levels.

Prisons

We have a great responsibility for the welfare of prisoners and just to shut people away and try to forget them will not resolve any of their problems - or ours in dealing with the situation. Colour would have a profound effect on those in prison; the pink cell research (and see Lighting) proved that some colours could be introduced which would have a calming effect on prisoners' minds, releasing fears and old patterns which they have accumulated throughout their lives. It takes time and cannot happen overnight, but a programme could be introduced and tested to see what effect it would have upon the inmates.

You would think that the worst thing that can happen to a human being is to be shut away, to lose one's freedom. As so many seem to return to prison having continued in the same vein as before once they get outside, it shows that the same tendencies can still remain. Our thoughts will always attract similar outside circumstances so it is a form of re-education that is required. I am aware there are many activities available for the prisoners but deep inside many still hold resentments, bitterness, guilt, anger, frustration ... one can go on with the list. They need to be able to get in touch with their deep inner feelings. We all have finer feelings and higher intentions; these need to be nurtured. The desire for change has to come from within; only then will change come about. Use of colour could start the process.

What most prisoners have lost is faith in themselves and others, and also feel the helplessness of everything: ' What is the point of it all?' I realise there are many people aware of what is being said here, but often the establishment can block trying out new methods. I have seen some remarkable results with the introduction of colour; where despair has turned to hope, deceit and deviousness to trust and faith. People find they have abilities within that they have never dreamed of. Everyone needs to feel needed at some point in their lives - then they can go out and help others in need. Prison can be a time of reflection, retrospection, transformation; a healing process taking place at many levels.

Dark murky colours should be avoided here - that includes browns, greys (except light grey, which could be included) dark greens, mustard yellows - and do avoid black; on the outside of the building it builds up a negative energy. The outside should be painted in royal blue with off white paint for windows etc. All corridors in the building should be a warm blue, the cell doors a peach mushroom colour, and inside the cells I suggest peach with off white and some green. If preferred, the corridors could be turquoise blue, complemented with a warm peach colour. The green chosen needs to be a pale green, as this increases the vibrations of an individual. Dining and workshop areas should have similar colours as chosen for the whole building; include some yellow but use it with discretion. Avoid blue here if all the corridors are already blue as there would be enough of that vibration within the building. When colours and lighting are used harmoniously together I feel it will bring about a psychological change in behaviour patterns.

Royal Blue in the Custody Suite

A new method has been introduced into the Police Force over the last few years due to the alarming rise in claims against the police. Now when a person is detained they are interviewed in the custody suite. The whole proceedings are filmed on a video after the person has been informed of his or her rights. At the touch of a button a computer will also give the officer in charge information as to whether that person has any previous convictions. The police say that this method protects both parties, recording the truth of what is said. According to the police the presence of a camera affects the detainee's behaviour dramatically; it also tends to dispel any aggressive tendencies they may have and the fact they are being filmed has a sobering effect, as the material can be used in court if necessary.

The colour of the custody suite is mainly blue and white. This will not only calm the person, but also encourage them to tell the truth, often surprising themselves! Here, technology and colour have been put to good use for all concerned and I quote from a report: "This method is cutting the time spent on the custody process and the standard towards a person's reception and handling has improved tremendously, as well as offering important safeguards for the officers."

Colour in Pubs

It has been noted that pubs with red walls are associated with a higher rate of fights, especially from male customers. Confrontations can arise over, for example, who uses the pool tables. It would seem that open plan pubs experience more fights than those who use partitions and screens. The study into crime in pubs was commissioned over a period of four years by different breweries and they found that two thirds of pubs have fewer than four fights a year between male customers, but 8% reported fights at least once a week; one in three resulted in substantial injuries. The influence of the managers is of great importance, for they are the ones to build up a reputation for fairness. How they treat their customers is all-important, and methods such as offering face-saving possibilities all help to defuse tense moments. The report does say that on average 5% of managers are assaulted every month. Of violent acts involving managers, 32% arise from refusal to serve disorderly customers; 30% from attempts to eject clients and 19% when managers intervene in fights.

Pubs need to avoid using red for the decor; paler tones or magenta will still give a warm, inviting environment and produce a different energy. Medium blue could be used for the partitions or screens and the pool table. Music excites; so careful monitoring of what is played is essential. Pubs might consider introducing blue lights placed in the ceiling. These could be turned on when required, and the customers might not even be aware of them unless they looked up at the ceiling, especially when they are interspersed with the rest of the lighting; but the manager would see the effect.

Complementary Notes

1. *A nanometer is the equivalent of one billionth of a meter; it is the standard unit measurement used to express wavelengths.*

2. *Superintendent Peter Bennett MA, MBA, A. Hague, LRSC, MIScT has now retired from the Police Force. He retired in 1994 after 30 years' service. He is now pursuing a Master Philosophy Research degree in Complementary Health Studies at the University of Exeter; he is also a tutor with the Open University Business School.*

Chapter 8: Part One - Shape, Form and Colour

When we study colour we realise it is a mental and psychological science and we respond through our sensations. Scientists today agree that we are immersed in a field of electromagnetic energy. The complete spectrum of electromagnetic energy contains sixty or seventy "octaves". It begins at one end with radio waves of exceedingly great wavelengths, proceeds through infra red rays, visible light and ultra violet. The wavelengths then get shorter and the spectrum reaches its other extreme in X-rays and cosmic rays. All this energy differs in length of waves and the frequencies and wavelengths are extremely accurate, and are accepted throughout the scientific world.

It is only more recently that scientists realise the potency of visual colour and that it affects all life form. Apart from a few scientists and clairvoyants the average person has, throughout the ages, never realised the power of the colour rays. Those who study metaphysics today have come to realise that the ancient civilisations were more aware of the healing power of colour and that a human being is a multi-faceted being.

One of the greatest mysteries is the rainbow. What is a rainbow? One cannot touch it as it has no material substance. When you try to approach it, it retreats; and when you go away, it follows you. Rainbows can also be seen in the water from a garden hose or when oil or petrol has been spilled on the ground, making us realise that the colours which are known as waves of energy are in everything we see, including not only plants and animals but also in and around us. The rainbow forms when light shines through moisture; the tiny drops of water in the air act like prisms which reflect back the light, and we see it as colour. Violet is on the inside of the bow and red on the outside.

Every drop of water mirrors the colours differently. Years ago I was given some water drop pictures taken with a high powered camera. Each picture was different in shape, form and and intensity; one was like a dove of peace and another like aeroplane wings. The red colour appeared more prominent than the others - this colour is known as the colour of the spirit of life, perhaps telling us how precious life is and showing the opportunities which are before us.

As we know, the rainbow appears as half a great wheel. The other half is there, entering the earth, but few people can see it. One of the well-known pioneers this century was Johannes Itten. He was a teacher at the famous Bauhaus School in Germany in the 1920's and interested in colour from a scientific and spiritual point of view. He devised a 'Colour Wheel' (see page 101) which has become a standard feature of art instruction throughout the world. His famous book "The Art of Colour" was published in 1961.

When you look at a 'Colour Wheel' *(See Complementary Note 1)* you will see a triangle in the centre. These are primary colours of pigments, called the primary colours since they cannot be created by a mixture of the other colours. Around the primaries in the shape of triangles are the three secondary colours, which are produced by mixing the primaries. For instance, Blue and Red produce Violet; Red and Yellow produce Orange; Yellow and Blue produce Green.

Around the triangles is the colour wheel and this is divided into twelve sections. Three of these are primaries and three secondaries; between each primary and secondary there is another colour Itten called the 'tertiary' colours, each tertiary being obtained by the mixture of a primary and a secondary. Thus according to Itten yellow and orange produce yellow-orange; red and orange produce red-orange; yellow and green produce yellow-green and so on. It is possible to create further subdivisions and today, as we know, many more colours are being introduced. The 'Colour Wheel' helps one to remember and visualise the colours quickly, forming a basis for working with colour pigments and paints.

Choosing Colours

When we choose colours for our environment we have to remember that a blue colour, for instance, when seen in the sunlight in a hot climate, will appear quite different from the same blue when viewed under the sunlight in the northern hemisphere. Electric light also changes the density of the colour. In winter time the light has more of the blue spectrum within it; that is why we sense a different atmosphere at these times even although the sun may be warm. In

England we call this an Indian summer. Colours change around us in nature as we go through the seasons; the depth and intensity of the colour rays are not the same.

Countries with a temperate climate do not tend to use the same vibrant colours as countries who have a lot of sunlight. This is also why temperaments differ; the amount of sunlight we receive affects us immensely, changing our personality and our whole approach to life.

Before deciding on colours you need to know what a room is going to be used for and whether it faces north, south, east or west. Keep to lighter colours for a dark room and rooms that have no daylight; try to keep them as light as possible. Lighting is also important here.

The BBC studios in London need a facelift! Some time ago I was interviewed on radio - the interview room had no daylight but only electric light and the colours were mainly dark. It looked dismal. I asked some of those who were working there if they felt drained tired and exhausted, and they said they felt it oppressive to work without daylight. They were often tired and felt exhausted. With the right colours and lighting (see Lighting) this can all be overcome. This situation applied to other radio stations I visited; so I say to those of you who are responsible for decorating these rooms do think of the staff! A colourful and lighter environment will have a very distinct effect; not only will they feel better but their health will improve.

At the Television Studios introduce turquoise instead of green for the so-called "Green Room". This colour is not only relaxing but calms the mind and the emotions. Research has shown that turquoise can help public speakers, actors and actresses - anyone who is nervous and has to speak in public.

How colour can create an illusion

Colour can be used with great effect to change the dimensions of a room. Warm colours make a room appear smaller whereas cooler colours give the impression of a larger space. Introduce a darker colour at the end of a long corridor or hallway and it will appear shorter; if you want to widen a corridor, use paler colours on the walls. Darker colours will make it seem narrower. One can always alter the shape and dimension of any space using colours in this way.

Archways on either side of a fireplace or elsewhere in a room can be made into a feature; the colour must blend with the overall scheme otherwise you lose the effect you originally wished to create. When a ceiling is painted in a darker colour and the walls in a lighter colour a tall room appears wider and lower; when the ceiling and carpet colours are similar the room will also appear wider and lower. If you want to create the impression of a high ceiling then use white or off white paint - this also increases the amount of reflected light that enters the room. A white ceiling creates a feeling of spaciousness; when you introduce a pale blue ceiling - which is calming and relaxing to the mind - you will feel a sense of vastness and of being free and unrestricted, because of its association with the blue sky.

The tone of a colour will change the mood and feeling of a room. Darker coloured carpets will always create a feeling of being 'earthed' or 'grounded', whereas paler colours create a lighter, more ethereal mood and feeling. As we change our outlook and attitudes we shall begin to use more of the lighter - and yes, in some cases, brighter - colours for carpets and curtains etc. Like Eastern countries we may take off our shoes when we come indoors; that is not just to keep the carpets clean but to leave at the door any negative vibrations.

Certain colours enhance each other and some colours repel each other when used together; for example, red when used with green has a calming effect on the red; blue will do the same for orange, and violet for yellow. Red and orange, orange and yellow, yellow and green, green and blue and blue and violet repel each other. (See information on Related Harmonies)

Ways of Using the Colours

One Hue Harmony

This refers to the use of one colour with all its different tints and shades. The choice can be either a warm or a cool colour, and it must complement the existing furnishings.

The many tones of light and dark colours can make the colour appear interesting, but this type of environment is very static. We need contrasts to keep our energy flowing. The idea has been popular but it could be one of the causes of the build up of stress in the environment (other factors, too, would have to be taken into consideration).

Related Colour Harmonies

Colours that lie next to each other on the 'Colour Wheel' are called 'related colour harmonies'. Interior designers take the two colours and use the shades and tints of the colours. To create a contrast they use several tones of the colours. When we understand colour as vibrations of energy, we see that placing together two colours that are next to each other on the Colour Wheel only creates an imbalance. For instance, when we place red and orange together there is far more of the red than the yellow (red and yellow make orange); see percentages below:

For example:			
	red and orange	1.5% is red	0.5% is yellow
	orange and yellow	1.5% is yellow	0.5% is red
	yellow and green	1.5% is yellow	0.5% is blue
	green and blue	1.5% is blue	0.5% is yellow
	blue and violet	1.5% is blue	0.5% is red
	violet and red	1.5% is red	0.5% is blue

In keeping with the laws of creation we need two colours together to create a third colour - for instance, to make orange we need red and yellow as mentioned above; to make green we need yellow and blue, and so on. To create harmonious environments we need energies that will polarise us; rather like electricity, with which the same laws apply. Even the introduction of white or grey within the colour scheme will only help to separate the two energies; they still will not create harmony. Should you wish to use related colours then introduce a complementary colour from either of the colours chosen; this will then create a balanced environment. We all need the warm and cool colours in any given space - to bring us harmony.

Contrast Harmony

This refers to the use of complementary colours together with their different shades and tints. I have already given many ideas on how to use colours in this way. When we look at the 'Colour Wheel' the complementary colours are opposite each other (see page 27 and the 'Colour Circle' page 28 which will give you more information.) Decide on your main colour and introduce different tones of colour, then complement it with its opposite or a contrast colour. Each of the illustrated contrast harmonies demonstrates the effect which results from the balanced use of contrasting and complementary colours.

Room One

The colours chosen for this room are red and pink; the red has been toned down to pink with two paler pinks, and green is the complementary colour. Green could be used to accent different areas in the room; when green paint is introduced into the room as well as pink only use this colour to, say, highlight any feature in the room.

Suggestions for use of this scheme: In the home, nursery schools, schools, doctors' and dentists' surgeries, clinics, psychiatric units.

Pinks represent safe, loving care

Greens are relaxing and peaceful

Room Two

Here, the colours are blue and magenta; the main colour is blue with its paler tones and the contrast colour of magenta. This colour scheme is very dramatic; the carpets and curtains in this colour would look warm and inviting. When using blue as the main colour you have to be careful that you do not create a cold feeling. The deeper blue could be used for skirtings and doors, and use the paler blue colours for the rest of the scheme. The curtains could also have some blue colouring within the pattern. These colours would look most effective in a university, as I have already mentioned in Colour and Education. You can reverse the colour scheme and have magenta as the main colour with all its tones, and use the blue as its complement. You may also use both colours with their paler tones for a big establishment - you would have more from which to choose.

Suggestions for use of this scheme: In the home, colleges, universities. High powered business establishments.

Blue - calming and relaxing

Magenta - uplifting

Room Three

The colours are violet and turquoise, with violet and its colour tones as a main colour . The turquoise brings it to life and gives a feeling of lightness and freshness. How you use the colours would depend on the mood you wished to create; but do remember that violet is a powerful colour.

Suggestions for use of this scheme: In the home, a hall of residence at a university for religious studies or in a hospice.

Violet is contemplative

Turquoise is calming and soothing to the nervous system.

Room Four

The colours are orange and blue, orange being the main colour. Use mainly the paler orange colours otherwise the effect could be too bright. The blue could be used for the doors, skirtings, window frames or just to highlight a particular area within the space.

Suggestions for the use of this scheme: In the home, schools, universities, offices, aeroplanes, reception areas for hairdressing salons.

Orange is creative

Blue is calming, relaxing

Do remember that plants, whether living or artificial, enhance any scheme. They add the finishing touches and should preferably be living plants, as they bring the life force energy into the environment and also transmute negative energy.

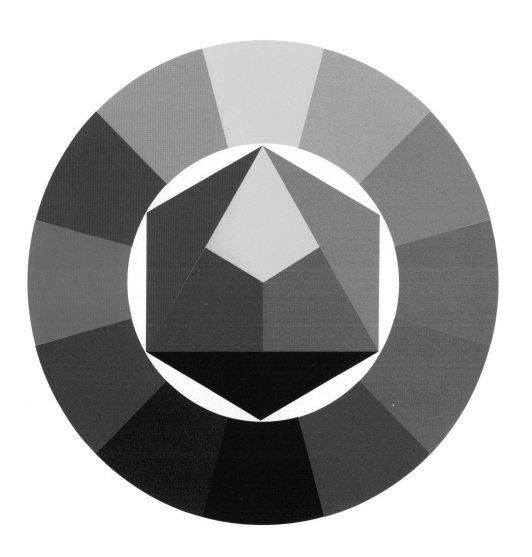

THE COLOUR WHEEL

by Johannes Itten

CONTRAST HARMONY

Refer to pagers 99 – 100

1

2

3

4

COLOUR AND PROPORTION

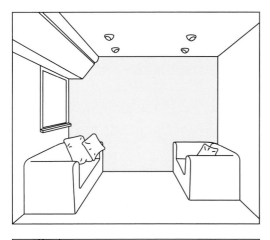 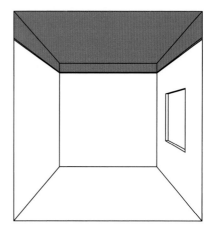

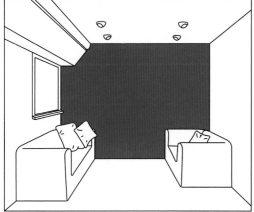 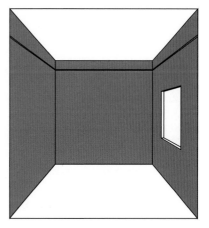

How Blue can make a room seem smaller, although blue is often thought of as a colour to increase the size of a room. It depends on the strengths of the colours.

The use of Red to alter the proportions of a room.

A Health Centre in Stockport

Some 40 children were recruited from Cale Green Primary School to produce this large and colourful mural. Working with an artist in their school and encouraged by Hospital Atrs, each child painted an image of a house. These were then assembled into an 18-foot townscape for display in the clinic's entrance

I think it is a wonderful idea to give children such opportunities; as they grow up they will never forget their involvement in a project of this kind, and it could encourage some of them to become community-minded when they are older.

Hospital Arts, Manchester, photo Helen Kitchen

St Mary's Hospital, Isle of White

Brian Chapman researched features of the local landscape, and included the Islanders favourite pastimes into his painting for this 30 feet curved wall at St Mary's Hospital, Isle of White.

Hospital Arts, Manchester, photo Helen Kitchen

Conservatory in a private home

Contrasting harmonies

A conservatory in a private home, illustrating the effects of using contrasting colours, the yellow from the warm spectrum balances the blue from the cool spectrum, bringing harmony to the environment.

Interior of Hotel - Chewton Glen Hotel

Illustration of shape form and colour.

The entrance hall to the hotel has predominantly been painted in one colour creating an area of spaciousness and it enhances the beauty of the interior, the coloured rugs create a feeling of warmth and ground the energies making one feel welcome.

The Meeting House - Sussex University

A circular building which has a moat around it, was designed by Sir Basil Spence, the architect of Coventry Cathedral.

Below the organ hangs the tapestry by John Piper, woven by the Edinburgh Tapestry Company in Scotland.

Michael Chapel -
Newton Dee, Scotland

"Edifices and buildings will begin to speak, and in a language of which people today have no sort of inkling."

Rudolf Steiner

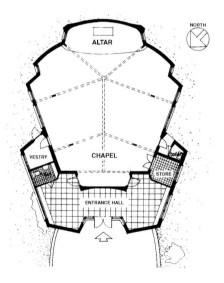

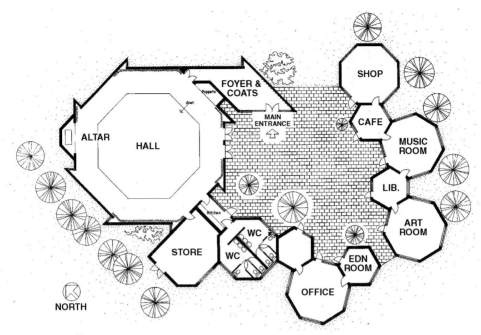

Cresset Hall,
Cresset Camphill Community,
South Africa

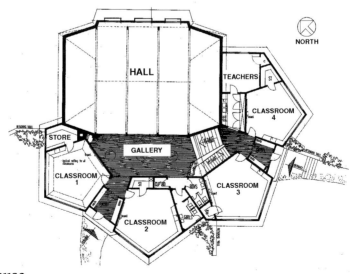

Karl König House,
Camphill Special Schools,
USA

Part Two - Shape, Form and Colour

Today most people are unaware that the shapes of our homes, buildings etc. have a profound effect upon us.

Houses are basically cube shape. This shape is identical to a square - it represents everything that is solid and durable, but the cube also symbolises limitation, feeling enclosed and confined. We can, if we are not careful, isolate ourselves in our homes, not wishing to go out and cutting ourselves off from our friends, taking no interest in what is going on in the wider world, looking at television and not participating in life.

When we look at the base of a cube it is square. This shape can support four triangles and it forms a pyramid. In sacred geometry the square symbolises matter and the triangle spirit and it looks like this: similar to the way we have built our homes.

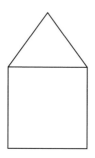

The cube and the square relate to the number four, as there are four sides; the four also represents matter, the four seasons, the four elements of which we are made (earth, water, air and fire). The triangle relates to the number three, and this number is important in all religions; as in the Trinity in Christianity. The roof of our square, cube-like houses is triangular and attracts the cosmic forces into our homes, buildings etc. It would seem the Ancient Egyptians knew what they were doing when they built the pyramids, leaving behind keys with which we can unravel the deeper meaning of life - and not only in shape and form. Properties with a flat roof are not drawing in the cosmic forces, so in such buildings the cube area builds up a lot of stress. The triangle represents harmony and perfect equilibrium, as its three corner points all lie exactly the same distance from each other; the corner points of a cube are in a state of permanent stress. To live in a pyramid shaped building in the present time would increase our energy and start the healing process for many of today's illnesses, but to live in this shape permanently would only disorientate us. Many people world wide have built pyramid structures to put into their gardens, big enough for a person to sit and lie down within for a certain length of time each day, with some good results. Like all such endeavours this needs more research.

It has been scientifically proven that we have five platonic solids which make up all shapes and forms which exist on earth. These shapes are in the four elements and we have these elements within us. The platonic solids are like building bricks; we can see some of these shapes when we look at a snowflake on a window pane before it melts. The shapes and forms it creates are magical. Mankind needs to become more aware of these energies and how they affect us. On pages 117 and 118 you can see how many patterns these forms make and how each corresponds to an element and a colour.

To live in high rise buildings above the seventh floor disturbs the energy around us, as we lose contact with the earth's energies. According to the Esoteric Teachings, this is because we have seven bodies of light around us and explains why so many people can feel unwell and so often complain of being stressed in this sort of building. Concrete buildings do not enable us to breathe through the aura. To live on or near places that have been rubbish dumps is unwise, as energy takes years to disintegrate. Never build on the top of an old cemetery; some would say it is sacred ground, but it is more than that. People who are very sensitive pick up all sorts of energies, and these places need healing.

In time to come we shall live in houses that have been constructed from natural sources. When I visited Vancouver in British Columbia, Canada, most of the houses were made of wood. They could easily be transported if you wished to move your home and demolished if a person wanted another type of house on the same land. The houses were warm and the design similar to brick built houses; for example, the front pillars of a Georgian type house were made from the trunks of the tree. Conservationists would say that the environment was being destroyed, but everything in life goes through its cycle; what matters is how we use natural resources and what they are to be used for. So many of the materials used today have an adverse effect upon us, and it is partly for this reason that so many people are tired and ill. Geopathic stress is now known to affect so many people. It is caused by our technological society, with too many electrical appliances in our homes emitting waves of electromagnetic energy into our auras. Even switching off the appliances does not stop some of the energy coming from the plug - we need to take the plug out of the socket.

Unfortunately most people do not realise that we are so much more than our physical body. We have an aura of light around us, whose existence is now recognised by leading scientists. We need to become more aware of the forces of nature - and that means creating homes and environments which are not only full of light, but which are healing us and the environment at the same time.

Architecture

As this century draws to a close we are seeing buildings that appear out of place in our environment. Some people feel as though the structures have come from outer space. Architecture reflects the society of the day and there are at present so many diverse ideas coming forward that are not harmonious that they have caused so much controversy everywhere. A modern town or city reflects its own energy, but trying to replace the old with the new will not create an harmonious environment, unless it blends with its surroundings.

Architects today are incorporating more of the sacred geometry designs - the five platonic solids - and want to create an wholistic environment. Bearing this in mind, architect James Mills (who can be contacted through the author) uses many of the sacred geometry patterns in his North London Hospice project. In his design there are triangles, rectangles, squares, pyramid shapes etc. and as far as possible only natural materials are introduced - this includes beach hand rails, bronze door handles and a sisal woven carpet. He took into consideration the people staying at the hospice, helping them to be aware of the forces of nature through the fabric and environment of the building and introducing fountains wherever possible inside, so that even if they could not see them they could hear them (running water is very healing to the emotions). Colour was important, as were their physical needs, including a hand held remote control which would enable a bed bound person to adjust the internal environment in the room. He emphasised the use of natural day lighting as well as full spectrum lighting, as the more light you have in a building, the more harmonious will be the environment created.

Some people today are experimenting with round houses. The Findhorn Foundation in the north of Scotland, a spiritual community formed many years ago, have built three round houses in wood. Living in this type of environment will create a feeling of freedom and expansion of ideas - as though you can do anything once you have made up your mind. But those ideas will only stay as ideas if one does not earth the building with, say, tables or mirrors that are square shaped. Copper on the roof will also help to earth the energy and can be very healing for the building's occupants. Copper will help to release stress.

The design of churches and cathedrals is based on sacred geometry and such buildings were created through the ages on ley lines - these are power points. They were also built with a spire reaching upward to attract the higher cosmic energies. Chartres Cathedral in France is a marvellous example of form and colour. The artchitects of the day must have been very intuitive and aware to build such a magnificent place.

Like all artists, architects' designs represent the soul expression of their being at the time of design. Only when mankind experiences a change in consciousness will we understand that outer forms reveal the splendour hidden within.

Inspired by Rudolf Steiner, Camphill Architects have built up their practice on the principle that a building should reflect the totality and dignity of the human occupants. The practice has emerged from the need to create buildings and environments which can support therapeutic work; helping those living within communities designed to cater for people with special needs.

If a building is to draw the soul qualities from us it must not only be aesthetically pleasing; its energy should also help people to aspire to a higher consciousness. The building itself should at the same time be at one with its immediate surroundings and with nature.

Joan de Ris Allen, an architect with the Camphill Trust, has produced a remarkable book called 'Living Buildings' (*See Complementary Note (part 2) 1*). It shows the progression in design of 50 buildings over 50 years, in 14 countries and all designed by the Camphill Trust Architects. Joan was herself the architect for Karl Konig House, a Camphill Special School in Pennsylvania, America, which opened in 1975 (see page 109). The design includes the pentagon shape for its form rooms and a rectangular shape for its hall, which pupils use for games and exercise. The building was built on two levels, blending in with it sloping landscape. The use of the pentagon shape (linked with violet - which lifts the consciousness and heals the environment) and the rectangle (linked with orange - the colour ray of purity, joy and creative expression) combines the two energies to act as a balance between body, mind and soul.

Another of the Camphill Centres, Cresset Hall, was built in South Africa and was opened in 1975. It is located in the Transvaal at six thousand feet above sea level. Its South African architect and artist, Monti Sack, designed the hall to be the centre point both outwardly and inwardly for the Cresset Children's Village. The focal point of the complex is eight hexagonal inter-connected classrooms clustered around an open courtyard. Its design is based on a regular octagon formed by fortress-like brick walls. This design acts as an anchor for the energies and gives the place strength and protection. (See page 109)

In Scotland, Camphill Architects designed the chapel at Newton Dee, Bielside, Aberdeen, which opened in 1989. The chapel is basically pentagonal, and to reach the entrance doors - which are built in solid oak - one crosses a paved forecourt with a virbela water cascade. Inside, coloured glass windows (created by Carl and Helen Wolff with the help of the Newton Dee community) depict the four kingdoms of nature. The chapel is a beautiful pink (see page 108)- it is as though the inside of the building is itself an expression of God's love in form.

For those of you interested in how to use the different platonic solids, I hope this book will inspire you. In time to come buildings will be like living organisms; places which will be so beautiful to behold they will express the Joy, Light and Soul of the people.

The positions in which we build our homes and places of work are important; the earth's energies do have negative lines of force that can be draining to all life forms. Studies in Austria under the direction of Dr Otto Bergmann (a professor at the University of Vienna) were carried out with doctors, chemists, physicists and biologists. They formed a working party and carried out tests on 985 people over a period of two years. To avoid a placebo effect the tests were organised so that neither the working party nor the subjects knew whether they had been sitting in a geopathically stressed area or a neutral area. However, those people exposed for only a few minutes to geopathic stress registered harmful effects in most cases.

Research has shown that too many electrical appliances in our homes also affect our energy fields. Living near to pylons or to any area which is generating a lot of electricity is harmful to our electro-magnetic field. Dulwich Health *(See Complementary Note - part two - 2)* is researching into all these areas and has introduced appliances which help counteract some of the energies, both internal and external, to which we are subjected.

Feng Shui, introduced from China and used extensively in Hong Kong, is based on encouraging the flow of good energy into and around a building. An expert can tell you whether, for instance, your chair or bed are in the right position for you to receive such energies. The position of the building is also very important; for example, a high rise block of flats can overshadow lower buildings and thereby affect their energy. Feng Shui enthusiasts put great importance on the correct placing of mirrors; not for reasons of design, but to improve the life force energy. Mirrors can deflect bad energies but can also draw good energies, such as those from water and mountains, to refract light. Mirrors can also be placed on unused doors to keep the flow moving throughout the office or home; but do remember never to hang a mirror so that it 'cuts off' your head - it implies that you do not want to know the reflection of yourself. Feng Shui experts lay great emphasis on plumbing, and suggest keeping WC lids closed in order to prevent money 'going down the drain'.

Very few people setting up business or moving house in Hong Kong would do so without seeking the advice of a Feng Shui expert. The name 'Feng Shui' means 'wind and water' - the wind links with the mind, the water with the emotions. The Chinese believe that when good energy flows through your home or your business you will have good health and prosper. Many Western people are now using these methods, which have aroused a lot of interest *(see Complementary Note (part Two) 3)*.

THE RIGHT USE OF ENERGY WILL BECOME THE MAIN FOCUS IN THE AGE TO COME.

The Five Platonic Solids *©

It is only possible to form regular crystal shapes from triangles, rectangles and pentagons.

From triangles we form the tetrahedron, the octahedron and the icosahedron.

From squares we form the cube.

From pentagons we form the pentagonal dodecahedron.

The Pentagonal Dodecahedron

When we take the six geometric forms which have the face of a house roof and base area exactly equal to that of the face of the cube, and then place these six forms on the faces of the cube (see picture below) we form a body called a pentagonal dodecahedron. This energy form brings balance and can change consciousness both in the outer form and within ourselves.

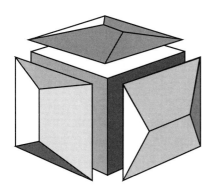 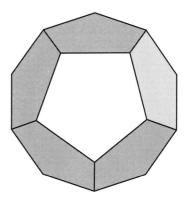

* 'Initiation' by Elizabeth Haich (*see Complementary Notes*)

© Reproduced by kind permission of the publisher

THE FIVE PLATONIC SOLIDS

Shape	Name	Number of faces	Element	Colour
	*Pentagonal dodecahedron	12	Ether	Violet
	**Tetrahedron	4	Fire	Red
	Octahedron	8	Air	Yellow
	Icosahedron	20	Water	Blue
	Hexahedron - Cube	6	Earth	Green

When we introduce the right colours and forms to any given space they have a therapeutic effect which is far reaching.

* Pentagonal Dodecahedron consisting of 12 equilateral pentagons.

** Hidden in the cube is the Tetrahedron, which has three equal sides; this represents harmony and equilibrium.

Complementary Notes - (part one)

1. *"Contrast Harmony" "Colour and Proportion" from "The Colour Eye" by Robert Cumming and Tom Porter - BBC Publications, 1990.*

2. *Mixing coloured lights does not produce the same result as mixing colour pigments.*

3. *Do remember that when applied to a wall or ceiling, colours chosen from a colour card will always appear darker, brighter and in some cases more luminous. Large areas of one colour create a more intense atmosphere, depending on the colour (pale colours do not give off the same effect). Today you can buy small sample pots of paint to try, so you can see what the colour looks like; better safe than sorry!*

   Interior designers use boards to illustrate the overall effect. They draw the design, introduce the colours and add small samples of the materials chosen so one can see what the finished effect will look like.

4. *Avoid using black in decor. We need a colour to feed and nourish us, and black has no light.*

5. *Choosing three colours for a home or most environments creates harmony, the three making the triangle which links with the body mind and spirit. When choosing colours for a very large building with several floors, choose three colours for each floor and carry one of these colours to the next floor, using different tones of the colour. This way you link the energy of each floor, creating a balanced and harmonious environment.*

6. *Always choose colours you like for your own home - after all, you are the one who lives there. Other people can suggest and give ideas but you need to feel good about the colours chosen.*

7. *When colours are chosen for a particular environment, whether a hospital, school, office, factory etc always take into account the activity that is taking place, for some colours are more conducive to some environments and activities than others.*

8. *It is important to have different shapes in any environment, as each shape has a meaning and creates a different energy - whether consciously or unconsciously, we do respond to it. All form has a colour vibration unique to itself.*

Complementary Notes - (part two)

'Living Buildings - An Expression of Fifty Years of Camphill'
by Joan de Ris Allen.
Published by Camphill Architects, Newton Dee, Bielside,
Aberdeen AB1 9DX.

'Intitiation' by Elisabeth Haich.
Published by The Seed Center 48, Briceland Road,
Box 1700, Redway, CA 95560, USA

To contact Dulwich Health write to them at
130, Gypsy Hill,
London SE19 1P1.

For information about Feng Shui contact The Feng Shui Association,
31 Woburn Place, Brighton BN1 9GA
(Tel: 01273 693844).

Chapter 9: Lighting

Lighting has come a long way since Edison introduced the lightbulb just over one hundred years ago. Today we take electric light for granted and it has changed our way of life. We can stay up all night to read or watch television - there are many who can work all night now such light is available. But the use of electric light is now having adverse effects upon us all. Most people have jobs which keep them indoors most of the day, and if there is very little light in the building, on goes the electric light. Over the years research has found that we all need natural light. Those who have to work inside day and night, in environments with electric light on all or part of the time will feel stressed and often tired, finding it difficult to concentrate, unless full spectrum lighting is used.

The three basic types of lighting used today are 'incandescent', 'fluorescent' and 'high intensity discharge'. The incandescent is usually pear shaped and we twist it into a socket; although it does give most of the visible spectrum the blue violet is missing, and most of the light output derives from the yellow red part of the spectrum. Research has shown it releases the energy mainly as infrared radiation and this sort of light is used mainly in our homes today - it is known as 'tungsten' lighting.

Fluorescent light is generated by non thermal mechanisms. It can produce different kinds of light depending on the substances these contain, producing a distorted spectrum of light which emits only a portion of the total spectrum. The cool white fluorescent light which is most frequently used is deficient in the red and blue violet colours we all need. This fluorescent light is used in schools, businesses and industry. One of the well-known pioneers into light research is Dr John Ott, who wrote a book 'Health and Light' *(See Complementary Note 4)*. Dr Ott has devoted many years to observing the effects of fluorescent light on plants and animals. In so doing he found there was a factor missing which enabled proper growth to take place, and he discovered that factor to be ultra violet light.

High intensity discharge - known as HID lamps - produce a very bright orange or blue light and are mainly used out of doors, in street lamps (orange) or as security lights (blue). Full spectrum lighting contains wavelengths of colour which have the ultra violet light included.

Full-Spectrum Lighting Research in Schools

A new Canadian study has found that putting full-spectrum lights into classrooms improves academic achievement. Attendance improves, pupils grow taller and it even lessens tooth decay. The study collected the results and health records of over 300 children at five similar suburban schools near Edmonton in Alberta and it took place over a two year period. In the schools with ordinary fluorescent light - in which the output of light is mostly from the yellow red part of the spectrum - pupils did not have the same vitality as those pupils attending the school with full-spectrum lighting. This study was carried out by Dr Warren Hathaway, a psychologist, and he presented it to the American Psychological Society. When electric light was first introduced no-one thought to consider its physiological or psychological effects. In Germany today fluorescent lights have been banned in hospitals and medical centres.

Because of the increase in illhealth worldwide there is a lot of research taking place and this is giving us knowledge and insight into what we have always known; that daylight is the best tonic for us all. It is important to reproduce this daylight where possible into our homes and our surroundings. The light used by most people within their homes does not carry the spectrum of light we need to stay well, and as more research is carried out around the world it increasingly demonstrates that the lighting we use has a draining effect on our energies.

During and after the last war tuberculosis was prevalent - this disease of the lungs was at the time virtually incurable. Part of the treatment was to bathe oneself in natural light as often as possible and pictures taken at the time showed people on verandahs in Switzerland, in bed but well wrapped up. It was even then known that they needed the ultra violet light to help start the healing process.

As long ago as the early part of this century, Niels R Finson of Denmark was a pioneer into light research. He founded the Light Institute for the cure of tuberculosis and he was awarded the Nobel Prize in 1903 for this work. Over 2,000 patients were treated with sunlight and artificial ultra violet light, with amazing cures. In every field pioneers come and go but it seems years have to go by before their work is recognised on a wider scale.

SAD - Seasonal Affective Disorder

Today there are many who are aware they become depressed as winter approaches, and this can continue until well into the spring. People can experience mood swings and a general feeling of fatigue, with no interest in anything. Sufferers tend to sleep more and yet still feel tired; they become lethargic, irritable and withdrawn in some cases. They tend to eat more during the winter months and can put on weight, often eating foods which they know are not good for them. This is known as Seasonal Affective Disorder - SAD, and sufferers are not to be compared with other depressives who suffer insomnia and lose weight. How does this disorder occur?

Light influences the 24 hour cycle. As the day draws to an end and the natural light dims the lack of light reaching the pineal gland starts the production of melatonin, a hormone which induces sleep. As it gets darker, more melatonin is produced and this makes us feel sleepy. In the morning when it is light, the melatonin production discontinues - and we wake up. This is how our body clock is synchronised to the 24 hour cycle. The pineal regulates appetite, fertility, growth and mood swings. It is when some people suffer from desynchronisation during the winter months when there is less daylight that they display Seasonal Affective Disorder. When spring comes SAD sufferers come to life.

In the northern hemisphere where there is very little light in winter - and in some places no light at all, and electric light has to be relied upon - the lack of light is known to stop a woman's menstrual cycle and it can also reduce the sex drive in both men and women. We need light to stay well - it is food for the mind, body and soul.

At the onset of winter when there is less light SAD can affect anyone.

It is said that 2 million people in England and 25 million in the States are affected by this disorder, but at last a cure has been found in the use of full-spectrum lighting. Jacob Liberman, in his book 'Light Medicine of the Future' *(See Complementary Note 5)* explains some of the research which has been implemented into understanding the cause and how those affected can be helped. Drs Wehr and Rosenthal initiated a research study for people who had the seasonal symptoms. They took two groups, having interviewed thousands of cases, and gave them light treatment for two weeks, six hours a day; one group had bright, full spectrum lighting and the other a dim, yellow light. Then each group was exposed for another two week period to the light source with which they had not yet been treated. The study was designed as a double blind so that none of the scientists apart from the primary researcher had any knowledge of the order of light treatments received by the patients. The patients, too, were unaware of which light source they were receiving.

The results were dramatic. All patients experienced improvements under the bright, full-spectrum light treatment while none showed improvements under the dim, yellow light, even though this colour is associated with the sun. Under the full-spectrum lighting some patients described themselves as 'being taken out of hibernation' and others reported feeling wonderful and able to resume normal activities.

NB   SAD symptoms can be so distressing that it has been known for people to need to give up their jobs; they find it difficult to cope with life in general.

The results of the above study not only established the existence of Seasonal Affective Disorder and its effective treatment but also created a whole new approach to treatment which has now been expanded into other areas. The above study has been documented within many different controlled studies internationally and light treatment is considered the treatment to choose for Seasonal Affective Disorder *(See Complementary Note 2).*

The benefits of sunlight and ultra violet light are endless. Light initiates a series of reactions which allow the body to produce vitamin D, which we need to absorb calcium - this is not to be compared with the vitamin D which is produced commercially. The pineal gland, which is the size of a pea, is situated in the middle of the brain and is affected by light changes; it affects our moods and sleeping/waking patterns. Too much artifical light can throw it out of balance.

Dr John Ott, well known for his experiments over many years, says that deluxe warm white fluorescents lacking in the blue-violet should be avoided absolutely. Too much ultra violet light is not good for us but he says we all need some to keep us well. Jacob Liberman also doubts the extremists in his book and poses the question; by cutting out all ultra violet light, have we gone too far?

Throughout the centuries, sun baths have been recommended for many conditions. Today, with the ozone layer causing concern, one can see how the pendulum has swung the other way. All life is moderation; for us to block out the ultra violet light will, I feel, only do us more harm in the long run. The early morning is the best part of the day to sunbathe, and even then only for a very short time. The weather news on English television now includes how long one should sit in the sun during the summer months, and information is given out for each day. We need to heed such warnings at the present time and to be wise about what we do.

For more information about full-spectrum lighting see the Complementary Note 1 at the end of this chapter.

Illumination in Interiors

We can introduce too much light or too little in our environment and either will alter the mood and feeling of our surroundings. Lighting will always change the density of the colours we use; the yellow orange effect of tungsten lighting which most people use in their homes will increase the density of the colours chosen. Red can appear to be orange, for instance. Fluorescent lighting reduces the amount of colour you see but it is only daylight lighting that will give you the true colours.

If you use a cool, fluorescent light in your bathroom and have a blue or green colour scheme, your complexion will look paler than it really is - so ladies, beware! Do not apply too much makeup in these conditions otherwise when you go out, you will not look natural!

In a bedroom, lighting needs to be soft ; if you like to read in bed, have a reading light nearby for that purpose, otherwise soft lighting can strain the eyes. Lampshades need to be chosen with care for the home or office; pale peach or pink colours give a soft glow and help us to relax but avoid green or blue shades, for blue is too cold and green is not good for our eyes. Yellow shades used in living areas will stimulate the surroundings; the choice depends on the mood you wish to create. Lights inset into the ceiling are the most effective and can give an overall light to any room; this is preferable to having a single light in the centre, which is often only turned on to enter the room. Wall lights are used more to give an effect than to give a proper light. The choice of where you place your lights is important; do make sure they are near enough for you to use when needed for reading, writing, sewing etc.

Table lights for the office have greatly improved and there are some attractive ones around. Do not just rely on overall lighting if you are involved in close work; you need a lamp nearby. Daylight screw bulbs are available and will reduce fatigue; only by trying them will you notice the difference. White lampshades with daylight bulbs are non stressful, but for some people they can look too cold. The choice depends on your colour scheme, as white reflects back the colours you have used.

Offices should not be too bright, as those present will find it hard to concentrate and will easily become tired. The difference to the atmosphere when full spectrum lighting is introduced is distinct, and the plants will thrive!

Hospitals

Night time can seem an eternity for any patient, but especially for those who are very ill. Usually a ward or a single room has some form of lighting kept on very low. A soft pale pink glow used for the early part of the night will help a patient to feel safe, secure and well cared for; later, a warm pale blue light will induce sleep and give off a healing energy for the patient. Green light should never be used; it is draining for all concerned, including the doctors and nursing staff. Children's wards need a pale pink light, again followed with a pale warm blue. Dimmer switches would be ideal for all rooms but especially those for children. Having different coloured lights in a hospital will give the staff a leeway of how and when to use them, whether separately or together ; a colour therapist can advise. When a patient is very ill both pink and blue can be used, in a ratio of 2 blue lights to 1 pink; as the patient settles for the night a blue light would be preferable. This also decreases restlessness, calming the mind which affects the body as it rests. Having been in hospital several times years ago, I am aware of the importance of having lights that make you feel all is well. Depending on the kind of lighting introduced, patients might not be aware of the colour but the staff will be aware of the effects.

I feel in time more coloured lights will be introduced to aid healing and it could become part of the nurses' curriculum to understand the deeper aspects of how and why colour affects us all so much. Too much of any one colour can reverse its positive action; initially you can feel wonderful and then later, drained. That is why I recommend having two colours in any given area, so that they can be used as mentioned above.

Another area where coloured lights would be helpful is in the waiting room. Often relatives are told disturbing news, and coloured lights would make a lot of difference in easing shock, or releasing the pressure and tension created by waiting for news. The lights can be turned on and off as and when required - otherwise daylight lighting should be used as the main lights for the room.

Prisons

Coloured lights in prisons could be most effective where there is a disturbance. Turning on blue lights would help to calm a violent situation, and these could be placed in the ceiling and only used when necessary. The blue light has a sedative effect and in this case turned on early enough the colour would build up a vibration which would in turn affect the atmosphere. When the disturbance has calmed, pink lights could be turned on - you will then find that prisoners would calmly go back to their cells without any further violence. It is in these institutions that colour could be most immediately beneficial. The cost might initially be high; but in the long run such use would pay for itself.

The pink prison cell proved to be successful in many cases, but using coloured light would be easier and just as effective - if not more so. The police force would not react so much against pink when the light method is used; many had objections to the Baker Miller pink colour, but the experiment gave insight into how colour does affect people and in which situations.

The workshop and dining areas in prisons could have lights to go with some of the other colours chosen for the rooms, and could be used in a therapeutic way. As prisoners receive the rays of light their whole system would be affected.

Industry

The lighting choice depends upon the colours used for the factory. Where these are mainly warm colours, then bright and high levels of illumination are needed, especially when the activity is focussed outwards. In cases where the work needs a lot of concentration then cooler colours are advisable for the main decor, such as soft blues, greens and turquoise. The lighting here needs to be softer and individually placed for the work in hand; too bright a light will be distracting.

It is interesting to see how our work activity reflects our inner being. People who are outgoing, sociable and love communication enjoy being surrounded by mainly warm colours, whilst those people who prefer to work on their own love a more peaceful environment and prefer the cooler colours. This demonstrates why it is so important to use complementary colours - one from the warm and one from the cool spectrum, to balance our energies.

Daylight lighting would be advisable for anyone doing intricate visual work. It would be less tiring and enable that person to see details more clearly. If intense illumination is required, according to Birren the surroundings ought to be suppressed in tone - this applies also to schools, hospitals, big offices etc.

Football Stadiums

Coloured lights could easily be used in football stadiums. Spotlights could be placed just high enough and out of sight, but turned on when required. Pink and blue lights could be used, with more blue than pink in a ratio of two to one. This back up lighting would calm an outburst should one occur. Wherever there is a large gathering and emotional tension is generated, there is always the possibility of fights which can get out of hand. Full-spectrum lighting would also stabilise the atmosphere, and should be used in cloakrooms and the players' rooms. Although research using the above method has not been carried out, I feel it would be very effective. Using light in this way would help in any large gathering; groups of people can panic and become emotionally disturbed very quickly, and coloured lights are far more effective than the simple use of colour.

Sports Centres

Here you can use many colours, but the changing rooms should be in soft tones. Wherever there is a danger area use orange instead of red, and blue to signify caution. Make sure people are not distracted by bright colours in areas where they need to be aware - for example, in swimming pools, a moment off guard can mean a life lost. Children learning to swim or who cannot swim very well should be encouraged to wear warm, bright colours as they can be easily seen in the water.

Sports centres could also look at having back up coloured lights, in a similar way as described for football stadiums. One major switch would be needed to control the colours for the building, with the addition of pink and blue spot lights around the place. Alternatively there could be one switch for pink lights and one for blue so either or both could be used. Pink light would calm any situation, and blue would stop any fighting or argument.

We all react to colour, but some people are not aware of why they react in a certain way. Reaction to colour is instantaneous; it affects our whole being, and it is only after the event we may analyse why we reacted in such a way.

Coloured Lights in the Environment

Unfortunately the signs ahead seem to indicate a society which is prone to violence. Coloured lights in underground stations - and any areas where it is known that trouble can occur - would be beneficial, although this would depend upon which colours are chosen. Discotheques which have swirling lights and loud music can disturb the psyche at deep levels, but the young and those who frequent such places do not want to know about the long term effects of subjecting oneself to such energies. A pregnant mother can do untold damage to her unborn baby by being in these frequencies, causing great stress to the baby which may manifest in the child later in many different ways.

Cities and towns lit up with lights that blink and swirl, displaying all the advertisements, will be open to some crime as when used in this way light affects people as they walk about. If the tendency is within a person to be disruptive, flashing lights will activate this tendency and, if given an opportunity, an outburst will occur. Even in the countryside where people generally feel safe and secure it is wise to have lights around a property which illuminate when someone is around. Here light acts as a good deterrent because a person can be seen. Creating a balance in today's environment is the concern of many, but I feel that prevention is better than cure. I have introduced mainly practical ways of how to use colour and light but always remember the power of thought; see your home, town and city in a blazing light in your mind. When many people work together in this way it is amazing to see the results - many who have tried it can tell you!

The difference between coloured lights and pigments

Colour pigment surfaces are only reflections of colour. Pigments give off the other colours they cannot absorb. As seen, for instance, in rooms, coloured pigment can alter the perception of space (page 103 and how blue and red seem to change the dimensions of a room). Under illumination, pigments change, and one can only tell what colour is being introduced by seeing the colour lamp or the source from which it came - hence the subtle and profound effect illumination can have on a person. Research has shown that colour, especially colour illumination, has an effect on all living cells; all the cells in the body are light sensitive to a lesser or greater degree depending on the person, and that is why we all respond in slightly different ways to colour.

Eventually, when more of mankind realises the benefits of colour and coloured light when used together with insight, knowledge and understanding, the results will be amazing. In places like hospitals, schools, prisons, institutions and in the market place generally this use will be cost effective in the long run and will lead to a healthier society.

Complementary Notes

1. *For further information on full-spectrum lighting write to:*
   Full Spectrum Lighting Ltd
   Unit 1, Riverside Business Centre, Victoria Street, High Wycombe,Buckinghamshire HP11 2LT. The company will also give you information about lamps to help S.A.D.

2. *Write to the S.A.D. Association, PO Box 989, London SW7 2PZ enclosing a SAE and they will send you an information leaflet. They recommend a high intense bright white light which has more blue than ultra violet light in the spectrum, and TRUE - LITE, which is a general purpose fluorescent tube that stimulates the full colour and has the beneficial ultra violet spectrum of natural daylight.*

3. ***Blue lights*** *are now being used in hospitals world wide for babies born with jaundice. This usually affects premature babies, and if not treated can result in brain damage or death. Before it was discovered that blue light was so effective, doctors had to give the baby a complete blood transfusion. Today blue or full-spectrum lighting is used on the baby for several days, and effects a quick recovery.*

4. ***For more information on light research*** *refer to 'Health and Light' by John N. Ott, published by Ariel Press, Columbus, Ohio, Atlanta, Georgia, USA.*

5. ***References to light studies;*** *'Light Medicine of the Future' by Jacob Liberman, O.D. PhD, published Bear and Company, Santa Fe, New Mexico. He has worked with more than 15,000 individuals ranging from the learning disabled and physically/emotionally traumatised people to business executives and Olympic athletes, treating patients with coloured light through the eyes.*

6. ***The Crystal Box;*** *ideal for therapy rooms, meditation and in the home to give a relaxing atmosphere, the four inch square box has a 15 watt bulb inside and it comes with a choice of twelve colours (crystals are not supplied). The lid has an aperture so the light can shine through the colour filter of your choice into a clear quartz, which radiates the colour. Rose quartz can also be used with a pink filter; this gives a wonderful,*

warm glow, soothing to any atmosphere. The boxes are available from the author.

7. *A pyramid lamp, whose measurements are in direct proportion to the Great Pyramid at Giza and on which different coloured stained glass can be placed, is available from Philip Dawes, 5 Brentmead Place, London NW11 9JD. Tel: 0181 201 8714.*

8. *I have mentioned different ways of using pink and blue lights. This is because pink calms the emotions and affects the muscular system, and blue calms the mind and reduces the blood pressure. Do bear this in mind if you want to change the ratio of how you use them.*

Chapter 10: Light and Colour in the Future

In the next millenium light, electricity and power will be the scientists' main areas of research and they will be looking into how and why energy affects us so much. Today colour energy around the human body can be photographed with special equipment but in time to come, more will be known about the etheric body around each person. Esoteric teachings tell us that this Body of Light holds the key to our state of health and its study will eventually lead to preventative medicine. We are living in exciting times, as so much knowledge unfolds about our universe and ourselves. Information which has remained dormant for years is now surfacing as the spiritual consiousness of the world is rising. The world of chaos in which we currently find ourselves living will eventually change; the old forms will gradually go to make way for a new way of thinking and being.

Colour is the healing power of the present and our future and it will be used in many ways; as our understanding of these powerful forces unfolds, we shall heal ourselves.

In the future we will be able to turn on the shower and, at the turn of a switch, decide on the colour of our choice in order to have a colour shower. Research into these areas has been under way in Germany for some time. Colours will gush forth from the sides of swimming pools and this discovery will be used initially in a therapeutic way, for specific ailments. Later I feel these methods will be introduced into all major swimming pools but training will be needed into how to use colours in this way.

Dr Peter Guy Manners uses sound in his swimming pool to help patients. Sounds and colours share frequencies - scientists have already proved that the seven colours of the spectrum, the seven notes of the musical scale and the seven glandular systems have a direct, innate relationship. *Dr Peter Guy Manners may be contacted at Bretforton Hall Clinic, Bretforton, Vale of Evesham, Worcestershire WR11 5JH.*

Soon we shall see fountains of colour in the market place, some with just one colour and others with all the rainbow colours pouring out of them. Most offices and establishments will have some form of fountain in the building which emits these colours. These fountains will be personally very healing.

People will feel calmer as they sit near them and watch the colours pour through the water like cascades of light. Smaller fountains will also become popular for offices; staff will start to relax more and the stresses we encounter today will eventually be a thing of the past.

Coloured light will be used extensively in the environment within shops, precincts and malls, restaurants, cafes, bars, banks, industry and so on - some of these I have already mentioned throughout this book. Research will prove that colour is most effective and creates a more peaceful and harmonious environment. As I have already mentioned, hospitals and prisons are already using some forms of coloured light for many reasons but gradually I feel its use will extend to other areas within these establishments. Schools could use it in the corridors and eventually more coloured light will find its way into our homes; by that time many will know that the choice of colours we surround ourselves with has a profound effect upon the whole of our being.

I never forgot my own experience with coloured light years ago. At a recording studio I visited to record a talk for a cassette there were coloured lights around the ceiling, and I was asked if I wanted them to be turned off. On the contrary, I thought they looked so wonderful I requested that they should stay on. Later, when I listened to my talk, there was a part I wanted to change, so I went back into the studio to re-do it. My voice was not the same; I had to record the whole lot over again. The lights in the studio had in the meantime been taken down, as they had originally been installed for a singing group. I realised the coloured lights had affected my energy and this had given a different resonance to my voice - the sound recordists could find no other explanation and were amazed.

You will find light fittings will start to change as people ask for more coloured lights in their homes. For instance, you could have a lamp with several sockets so you could use two blue light fittings, two pink light fittings and two white, and use them with a dimmer switch. These could then all be turned on at once, or separately at will, and the differences to your energy would be very noticeable. Theo Gimbel has introduced a lamp based on some of these ideas using several colours. Contact the Hygeia College of Colour Therapy, Brook House, Avening, Tetbury, Gloucestershire GL8 8NS.

Shapes and designs are important and must be kept simple. The wider use of spotlights has paved the way to the use of coloured light in the ceiling and in time, designers will introduce coloured light in more subtle ways, so that the bulb holder will be invisible, hidden by an overhang, and the ceiling itself infused with coloured light.

Our future is a vista of colour and here I have given only a few ideas, but in time designers will also become inspired and we shall find coloured light a delight, as it will beautify our homes and our environment.

As the public becomes more aware and realises the power of colour to affect health patterns then colour light therapy will become more universally accepted. Colour is already being introduced in this way. For a treatment, a colour therapist decides which colours a person requires and then a coloured light is focussed onto the person for a given length of time, over the area where it is needed or as a diffused light to cover the whole system. There are many techniques and methods which the therapist can use and results are already promising. Like our fingerprints, everyone's aura is unique and specific training is required together with an in-depth understanding of the colour rays. Eventually it will be possible to feed each person's data into a computer and have the correct colour frequencies diagnosed and given. It will entail a lot of extensive work and research to compile a system that is appropriate for everyone.

Dinshah Ghadiali, a Hindu scientist, produced a master work on colour therapy; he taught thousands and maintained that colour therapy involves a philosophy, a science and a technique of application.

I have been teaching colour therapy for many years and my own intuitive awareness has grown enormously, and continues to do so. When students realise the power of the colour rays and that they are pulsating light energies which lift us emotionally, mentally and spiritually they begin to develop and open up to a greater awareness which changes their whole lives. By introducing the many ways of using colour into their lives they develop their potential and everything becomes meaningful. I feel blessed to have been able to participate in their development.

THE ONLY WAY COLOUR WILL ADVANCE IS BY EXPERIENCE - KNOWLEDGE WITHOUT APPLICATION WILL NOT INCREASE AWARENESS.

Today so many people talk about the psychology of colour and becoming interested in the many ways in which colour can affect us, but are not very venturesome in trying out new ideas. It would appear that people only change their viewpoint should they become unwell, lose a loved one or their job; at such times they will look at anything and everything. It would be wiser to become accustomed to using new methods *before* such events occur, as we can then be stronger and more able to cope with such disturbing experiences. It is when our energy fields become low that everything seems to happen to us, first one happening and then another; then as our energy lifts everything starts to right itself. All this should tell us quite a lot - the magnetism around us attracts or detracts energy, depending on our own energy. **Prevention is better than cure.**

The visible spectrum has been virtually ignored except for the few torch bearers throughout time who have realised that the colour rays are powerful cosmic rays and that these rays give us life, light and warmth. Everything on earth is sustained by these colour rays; as research has shown, we hold the keys to our own future. How we use and tune into these rays determines how we come to know the presence of the *love and light* that created all life, and that through involution and evolution everything grows and changes like the caterpillar which eventually becomes the butterfly.

Master Omraam Mikhaël Aïvanhov, the Bulgarian Spiritual Adept (1900 - 1986) said it all so beautifully *(in 'Light is a Living Spirit' published Prosveta Editions, Dove Nest, Duddleswell, Uckfield, Sussex TN22 3JJ).*

"The sun's rays are the only things that are capable of sustaining, nourishing and increasing the flow of life in a man, *(meaning mankind)* but he has to learn to absorb them. If you open yourselves wholeheartedly to the action of the sun's rays *(the Master was referring to the sunrise)* you will feel that they begin to work for your regeneration and resurrection.

Light is everything. Light is the cause and the origin of the universe. Light is a spirit, a spirit that emanates from the sun - each ray of light is a potent force which penetrates and works on matter everywhere.

You can picture this incandescent light as purple, blue, green, yellow, orange or red but it is preferable to picture white light, for white light combines and unites all the others. White light can give you the omnipotence of purple, the peace and truth of blue, the wealth and eternal youth of green, the wisdom and knowledge of yellow, the health, vigour and vitality of orange, the activity and dynamic energy of red. But above all, picture white light to yourself. When you reach the stage of concentrating completely on light, when you sense it as a vibrant, throbbing, quivering ocean of peace, happiness and joy, then you will also begin to sense it as a perfume, and as music, that cosmic music which we call the music of the spheres, the song of the whole universe."

Index

Colour and Health Care

Colour - its Application Within the Commercial Environment

How Colour Can Reduce Violence and Influence Behaviour Patterns

Bibliography for further reading

Aïvanhov, Omraam
Mikhaël: 'Light is a Living Spirit' : 'Toward a Solar Civilisation' ; Pub. Prosveta Editions, The Doves Nest, Duddleswell, Uckfield, Sussex, England TN22 3JJ

Allen de Ris, Joan: 'Living Buildings, an Expression of Fifty Years of Camphill'; Pub. Camphill Architects, Newton Dee, Bielside, Aberdeen, Scotland AB1 9DX 1990

Birren, Faber: 'Colour Psychology and Colour Therapy'; Pub. University Books. Imprint of Carol Publishing Group, New York, USA.

Babbit, Edwin S: 'The Principles of Light and Colour'; Pub. Citadel Press 1967. Imprint of Carol Publishing Group, New York, USA

Cumming, Robert &
Porter, Tom: 'The Colour Eye'; Pub. BBC Books, London, England 1990

Dinshah D.:   'Let There Be Light' ; Pub. Malaga NJ Dinshah Health Society 1985

Gimbel, Theo: 'Healing Through Colour'; Pub. The C.W. Daniel Company Limited, 1 Church Path, Saffron Walden, Essex, England 1980

Haich, Elisabeth: 'Initiation'; Pub. Seed Center, PO Box 1700 Redway CA 95560 USA 1974

Irlen, Helen: 'Reading by the Colours'; Pub. Avery; Distribution via Media Service, c/o Biblios Ltd, Star Road, Partridge Green, Horsham, West Sussex, England.

Kilner, Walter J.:   'The Human Atmosphere'; Pub. University Books. Imprint of Carol Publishing Group, New York, USA

Lacy, Marie Louise: 'Know Yourself Through Colour'; Pub. The Aquarian Press 1989. An imprint of Harper Collins Publishers

Liberman, Jacob: 'Light, Medicine of the Future'; Pub. Bear & Company, Santa Fé, New Mexico 1991

Ott, John N.: 'Health & Light'; Pub. Ariel Press, Columbus Ohio, Atlanta Georgia, USA

Senior, Peter &
Croall, Johnathan: 'Helping to Heal, the Arts in Healthcare'; Pub. The Gulbenkian Foundation, London, England 1993

Steiner, Rudolf: 'Colour'; Pub. Rudolf Steiner Press, London, England 1982

Wood, Betty: 'The Healing Power of Colour'; Pub. New York Destiny Books 1984

Copyright – acknowledgements

My grateful thanks to the following for permission to quote or use artwork for the book:

Professor Harry Wohlfarth, University of Alberta, Edmonton, Canada

Guy Eades, Director of the Healing Arts at St Mary's Hospital, Isle of Wight

Peter Senior & Johnathan Croall, 'Helping to Heal, the Arts in Healthcare'

Blackthorne Medical Centre, Maidstone, Kent

Faber Birren 'Colour Psychology & Colour Therapy'

Superintendent Peter Bennett (now retired) 'The Use of Baker-Miller Pink'; Pub. International Journal of Biosocial & Medical Research - Volume 13 1991 PO Box 1174 Tacoma WA 98401 - 1174 USA

James Mills, The North London Project

The Meeting House Chapel, University of Sussex

The British Dyslexia Association

Robert Cumming & Tom Porter 'The Colour Eye'

Joan de Ris Allen 'An Expression of Fifty Years of Camphill'

Full Spectrum Lighting Ltd

S.A.D. Association

Jacob Liberman 'Light, Medicine of the Future'

Dr Peter Guy Manners, Bretforton Hall Clinic

Elisabeth Haich, 'Initiation'

Omraam Mikhaël Aïvanhov 'Light is a Living Spirit', Prosveta Editions

The Institute of HeartMath
14700 West Park Avenue, Boulder Creek, Ca 95006 USA

British Dyslexia Association
98 London Road, Reading, Berkshire, England RG1 5AU

Dulwich Health
130 Gypsy Hill, South London, England SE19 1P1

Full Spectrum Lighting Ltd
Unit 1, Riverside Business Centre, Victoria Street,
High Wycombe, Buckinghamshire, England HP11 2LD

S.A.D. (Seasonal Affective Disorder) Association
PO Box 989, London, England SW7 2PZ

Feng Shui Association
31 Woburn Place, Brighton, England BN1 9GA

Blackthorne Medical Centre
St Andrew's Road, Maidstone, Kent, England ME16 9AN

Philip Dawes (Pyramid Lamps)
5 Brentmead Place, London, England NW11 9JD

Wolodymir Radysh MFA., DA., FIAL., FIACS
Camphill Architects
Newton Dee, Bieldside, Aberdeen, Scotland AB1 9DX

Dr Peter Guy Manners MD., DO., LBCP., PhD., FICTM., DD., MHMA
Bretforton Hall Clinic
Bretforton, Vale of Evesham, Worcestershire, England WR11 5JH

Theo Gimbel DCE., MIACT., NFSH., MLHRC., Cert. Ed., BRCP
Hygeia College of Colour Therapy
Brook House, Avening, Tetbury, Gloucestershire, England GL8 8NS

Professor Harry Wohlfarth MFA., DA., FIAL., FIACS
University of Alberta, Canada T6G 2T4